love more,
FIGHT LESS

COMMUNICATION SKILLS EVERY COUPLE NEEDS

love more,
FIGHT LESS

A RELATIONSHIP WORKBOOK
FOR COUPLES

GINA SENARIGHI, PhD, CPC

NEW YORK

Copyright © 2020 by Penguin Random House LLC

Published in the United States by Zeitgeist, an imprint of Zeitgeist™, a division of Penguin Random House LLC, New York.

penguinrandomhouse.com

Zeitgeist™ is a trademark of Penguin Random House LLC

ISBN: 9780593196656

Cover art © igor kisselev/Shutterstock.com
Interior art © Bariskina/Shutterstock.com
Book design by Stacy Wakefield Forte

Printed in China

7 9 10 8

First Edition

TABLE OF CONTENTS

COMMUNICATION

*is the foundation
of any relationship*

IN LIVING ROOMS, restaurant booths, cars, and text threads around the world, couples attempt and avoid difficult conversations every day. The topics can run the gamut of a relationship, ranging from wedding and vacation plans to accusations and apologies. These discussions, whether complex or delicate, become opportunities for communication or miscommunication.

For 10 years, I've been supporting couples all over the world as a therapist and coach both individually and by running couples retreats and communication workshops—and I've seen it all. From couples colliding over household chores to marriages nearly ending over punctuality (or lack thereof!), my clients' concerns have been diverse. However, I've noticed several repeating themes and learned that even skilled communicators can struggle with conflict in their most intimate relationships.

Here's the problem: most of us just haven't been taught how to navigate conflict in healthy ways. Our role models failed to show us how to handle resentment, accountability, and misunderstanding. These early experiences create a set of default communication patterns we carry forward in adult relationships. And for most of us, those defaults could use a tune-up.

Believe it or not, resetting these defaults and learning new skills can actually be fun. I've helped thousands of couples by teaching them how to communicate effectively and lovingly—even in tense situations.

When clients arrive at my retreats, they've often lost each other under a pile of missed connections, rejections, and misunderstandings. Most of them have been fighting about the same seemingly small things for years. They're drained and sometimes losing hope. They ask me, "Is change really possible? What if we're just fundamentally different in some way? What if this is just how we are?" I tell them, "Change is always possible." And it is, if they're open to releasing the tension and learning simple skills to move forward in new ways.

As I work with couples, we build new skills to self-reflect, take personal accountability, and repair past hurts. As we clear the emotional debris, we move forward with fortified trust and compassionate boundaries. Using their new skills, couples become more comfortable in moments of tension and more confident managing emotional reactivity without withdrawing, escaping, or lashing out.

This workbook features simple tools you can use to reset your defaults for deeper understanding and meaningful connection. The skills I teach work for every relationship status—married, dating, and even "it's complicated." Gay, lesbian, straight—every partnership needs healthy communication skills to survive. While new research shows us there are some unique challenges and strengths in communication for same-sex and queer couples, the bulk of the studies show that all of us—regardless of orientation—default to the same communication patterns. And that's where the strategies I teach will come in to play.

Essentially, as couples love more, they fight less. And the fights they have are far less harmful.

There is nothing more rewarding than seeing couples become conflict confident, moving from resentment to relaxed warmth. Their shoulders soften and their smiles return as they integrate humility and gentle humor in even the tender moments. They know the answer isn't being free from conflict; instead, it is using skillful communication practices to move through disagreements and misunderstandings quickly. They use conflict as an opportunity to deepen their bonds respectfully.

why couples fight

Over 90 percent of my clients say they want to overcome communication issues. They either hate the way they fight or they don't know how to have healthy conflict, so they avoid tender topics until they erupt—which rarely reaches resolution. Instead, the resentment has built up and created distance and discord, and now they can't see a way out. Maybe that sounds familiar to you? Communication, I tell my clients, can ruin a perfectly good relationship.

When I ask my clients how often they communicate, most feel they are never more than a second away from their partner because they can text, email, and message each other almost constantly. In today's society, people experience both the immediate high of connection and a more intense erosion of connection than in any era before. Why? This hyper-connectedness breeds opportunities for misunderstanding tone and content, which increases the likelihood of harmful communication.

Plus, the extreme time constraints faced by modern couples make it easy to become ships passing in the night. It's too hard for most couples to set aside time for the connection they want—let alone to resolve the

BE PRESENT

If you're practicing with your
partner, do a quick scan of both of
your physical and mental states.
Does one of you feel hungry or
tired? If yes, address those basic
needs first. Make an appointment
to regroup if necessary.

conflict they know needs attention. Most couples I work with spend less than an hour each week fully present with each other.

Too much and too little communication are killing our relationships. Fortunately, we can remedy that. Using the tools in this guide, you can shift your patterns and integrate effective communication skills into the relationships that matter most.

FIGHTING & INEFFECTIVE COMMUNICATION

When couples tell me they want to focus on improving communication, they really mean they want to learn to fight less. And while conflict can be distressing if it's not handled well, it is actually a natural and necessary part of being in a relationship.

The trick is learning to navigate conflict with care. Most fighting isn't constructive and can result in real damage to your connection. We'll focus a considerable amount of attention on the ways you can manage conflict to bring you closer rather than deepening the divide.

For example, when my clients Matt and Kevin first walked through the door, they said they had "trouble communicating." They seemed to be communicating well, but on closer inspection, we uncovered an issue. Matt had been raised by detached parents and was in the habit of avoiding his needs. He either tried to "set them aside" or employed passive-aggressive tactics that Kevin usually missed or misunderstood. Matt was frustrated, and Kevin felt like he was constantly disappointing his partner.

When Keith and Samantha came to me, they thought they might have to call it quits. Samantha especially was at her wit's end, telling me that she couldn't believe how poorly their conflicts went when in her day job she was brokering international peace. "I have the skills out there, but I just can't help myself when it's with Keith," she said. For so many of us, our best communication skills might show up at work, but we just can't seem to take them home.

Another couple, Sasha and Dayton, had been together for 18 years when they landed on my couch. "We've built a beautiful life together, but when it comes to sex, we're so stuck we can't talk about it without screaming or crying," they shared. They, like so many couples, can navigate most of the complexities of life just fine, but when it comes to one particular subject, they shut down.

Communication conflicts in intimate relationships are uniquely bewildering. Most of us experience intense and chaotic conflicts with the people we care about most. The good news is, we just need better skills. With simple reflection and the skills in this workbook, you can transform your partnership's conflict patterns.

how to use this book

Workbooks are an excellent tool for personal growth and development. They help readers incorporate learning into actionable change in real time. This workbook will give you tools and resources to master effective communication and guided reflections so you can tune up your interpersonal communication skills.

You can work through the book on your own or, ideally, with your partner. The exercises are designed to bring you closer and build better understanding to move you forward. Even readers in relatively low-conflict relationships will benefit from these exercises, as they deepen connections in the partnerships that matter most.

This book is organized into two parts. The first part outlines six critical areas to focus your communication tune-up. Each area will help you identify spaces for you to grow your skills with clear activities to share with a partner.

The second part walks you through relatable real-life scenarios that commonly cause conflict for couples. These are issues I see coming up time and time again as I work with a wide variety of couples. We'll use the communication skills learned in part one to help you work through these potential conflict zones.

SETTING EXPECTATIONS & TIPS FOR SUCCESS

Before you begin, I want to share six important tips for success to keep in mind as you move through this book.

commit

In order for these activities to work, both partners need to be engaged in learning. As you move through the activities in the book, be sure both you and your partner have had ample time to reflect. Before sharing your responses, check in to ensure you're in the best possible space for sharing compassionately. You know you're probably not in the best mindset right after a rushed commute or a stressful day at work, for example.

breathe

Take your time as you move through this book. Change is often a slow process. Forcing your way through the material will not bring about more successful or sustainable changes; in fact, it could do the opposite.

think long game

Reworking long-held communication patterns is a long-game growth process. Remember: there are no time limits set, and because it's a workbook, you can return to it after taking breaks to digest the information in each section.

practice, practice, practice

It would be really lovely if you could complete a workbook and immediately change patterns for good. However, change takes practice. Commit to engaging in this work on a regular basis.

patience, patience, patience

Don't be disheartened if you experience some setbacks as you implement changes. Be as patient as you can with yourself and your partner. Do your best to return to the skills outlined here, and over time you will see powerful changes in your communication patterns.

overcome limiting beliefs

When we face new learning, three common limiting beliefs often get in the way of growth. In order to create change, we must first be open to it. I want to warn you about these beliefs in case you encounter them as you work on your connection.

→ **"I ALREADY KNOW THIS."** It's true—some of the things we will go over may be lessons you have heard in the past. The simple truth is we rarely take time to intentionally apply the truths we know of relationships to our own lives or practices. If you stay open and curious as a learner, you will find ways to integrate the lesson and you may learn at a deeper level this go-round. Instead of saying, "I already know this," ask yourself, "What can I learn from this?" Try to see the information from a new angle or with new appreciation.

→ **"WE'VE ALREADY TRIED EVERYTHING."** A similar limiting belief can come in the form of "I already tried this" or "This won't work for me." Instead, remember to stay open and curious as a learner, and ask yourself, "How can this work for me?" Even if you have tried something similar before, you are a different person than you were then, and your ability to move toward happiness may be different now. Challenge yourself to try it anyway.

→ **"IT CAN'T BE THIS SIMPLE."** Finally, one of the other limiting beliefs clients encounter in this work is "This is too simple." Strange but true, the ease of these practices leads many couples to take a relaxed approach when applying them. When we think skills are too simple to make a real difference, we're totally wrong. True meaningful connection is made in the smallest of moments in relationships. Overlooking these tiny opportunities for connection or understanding leads to long-term decay in partnerships. This book is filled with tiny tweaks you can make to see real change in your relationship patterns. Don't let the ease fool you—staying committed to this process will help you get and stay clear.

part one

· · · · · ·

EFFECTIVE COMMUNICATION SKILLS

this section is divided into six chapters, each offering five skills to practice on your own and with someone you love. We'll start with practices to build self-awareness to improve your internal communication skills and set a foundation for better connection in your partnership.

We'll cover the most common problems in talking and listening, as well as the best ways to resolve conflict, repair harm, and make up after tough times. We'll work to deepen your intimacy and trust for longer-lasting passionate connection. And we'll finish up with a section designed to help you explore healthy boundaries.

These skills will not come to you overnight. As with anything new, you must keep practicing to master them. Before you begin, take note of your physical and mental state. Address any needs for rest, water, or food. Set aside a distraction-free space to do this work. Put away screens and phones, and make this a time for just the two of you.

Finally, don't rush. Give yourselves lots of space to try out new and different ways of being together as a couple.

1
····

SELF-AWARENESS

THE RELATIONSHIP we have with ourselves sets the foundation for every other relationship we have. So, before you can start working on relationships with others, let's use this chapter to increase understanding of your individual default settings, grow skills to manage intense emotions, and interrupt patterns that keep showing up in your relationships.

building awareness of your defaults

GOALS

→ Identify early relationship lessons and teachers.

→ Increase understanding of our default expectations, patterns, and reactions.

→ Begin intentionally choosing which patterns need updating.

Without realizing it, we've all absorbed thousands of tiny messages about how to act in relationships from our family, community, and early relationships. Over time, our relationship role models and first romances teach us valuable lessons about how to set boundaries, show respect, commit to a partnership, and care for each other.

Those lessons combine to set our default norms and expectations. They help us grow certain strengths and create reactive patterns we often carry for many years without even noticing.

For most people, some of these defaults work well and some of these defaults hold them back. The good news is that we aren't limited by these patterns. With guidance and practice, we can learn new skills that will ultimately improve our relationships.

ACTIVITY

Use the questions below as journal prompts for timed writing sessions. Set a timer for five minutes, and write a response without editing or stopping until your time is up. Repeat with another prompt.

Once you've completed a few questions, review your writing and select a few phrases or sections you feel comfortable sharing with your partner. Take time to share with each other. You and your partner may want to practice the listening skills in chapters 2 and 3 before sharing.

family

What did my family teach me about boundaries and conflict resolution?

What did I learn
about anger and
emotional reactivity
from my family?

What did my family
teach me about
apologies and
forgiveness?

early life experiences

What did my early
life experiences,
particularly
friendships,
teach me about
boundaries and
conflict resolution?

How did my early
life experiences with
forgiveness and
relationship repair
inform the way I act
in relationships?

How did my early life
anger and emotional
reactivity inform
the way I behave in
conflicts now?

early love life

What did my early
love life experiences
teach me about
forgiveness and
relationship repair?

What did my early
love life experiences
teach me about
boundaries and
conflict?

community

What were the community norms about boundaries and conflict where I grew up? How did they work for me or challenge me?

DISCUSSION NOTES

Take time to share your learning with your partner. Which of your defaults work well together? Which need a tune-up?

identifying reactivity

GOALS

→ Learn to tune into your body's cues that tell you you're feeling reactive.

→ Practice connecting with your reactivity.

→ Begin the process of slowing down when reactivity sets in.

We all experience emotional reactivity when things get tough. We get angry or fearful or feel hurt, and we're likely to lash out or withdraw in defensiveness. Too often our reactive emotions lead us to self-sabotage or to harm our relationship.

To change the way reactivity shows up in our lives, we have to know when it's coming. Let's start by tracking down the root of your reactions.

This is arguably the most important step to resolving issues of intense emotional reactions. It is also one of the most difficult because it relies on an honest self-assessment and a willingness to explore unpleasant emotions—even while in the midst of them.

For most people, our body tells us reactivity is present well before we realize it cognitively. Let's start by identifying your body's cues that you're experiencing reactive emotions. Once you can recognize them, you can interrupt them before your reactivity gets the better of you.

ACTIVITY

Think of a current or recent scenario where you experienced reactivity. Draw the scenario, key players, and setting below.

Mark and note the sensations you feel in your body as these scenarios play out. Do you feel heat or cooling sensations? Are parts of you numb? Where do you feel tension or tingling in your body? Which parts of you are clammy or sweaty?

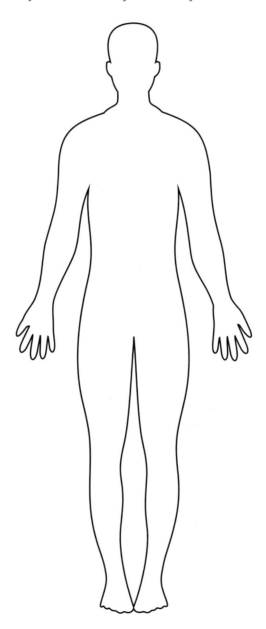

Our bodies often give us the first signals emotional reactivity is beginning—far earlier than our minds become aware. By paying close attention to our body's cues, we can better manage our responses and choose action that won't leave us regretful later.

My body tells me I'm feeling reactive by . . .

DISCUSSION NOTES

Notice when and where it is easiest for you to tune in to your body's cues. Try to find a space and time to practice checking in with your body once per day.

learning to interrupt reactivity

GOALS

→ Practice several self-soothing techniques.

→ Apply techniques in moments of high emotional reactivity.

Once we know what reactivity feels like in our body, we can begin to slow it and interact with it in different ways. Self-soothing techniques are simple practices we learn as children to help calm ourselves when emotions run high.

As we get older, most of us stop practicing intentional self-soothing when we're feeling jealous, insecure, defensive, or angry.

It can be too easy to start relying on our partners for all of our emotional support when we're triggered. While it's wonderful if they are a source of positive connection, warmth, and kindness, it's important that we can provide the support we need for ourselves as well. Otherwise, we can put too much pressure on our partners and/or isolate ourselves from the other supports we need for a healthy, fulfilling life.

SELF-SOOTHING TECHNIQUES

There are lots of ways to practice self-soothing. The first step is to put space between you and the anxiety-producing trigger. You might need to walk away or leave the room to avoid emotional reactivity and stop yourself from falling into the same old pattern. Then use any of the self-soothing techniques below to help your body and mind come back to baseline. Try to find ones that work best for you.

mindful breathing

Mindful breathing should be our first response to any crisis. Think of it like the EMT showing up at an emergency scene. It can help us get through the immediate situation and, just like the EMT, take us to a more secure place where we are able to address the problem.

There's not one single way to breathe mindfully. Experiment and find a technique that feels comfortable and soothing for you. One popular technique goes like this:

1. Start by closing your eyes and breathing normally.

2. Imagine that all of your anxiety, fear, and stress is a cloud that's floating in the air around you like a toxin.

3. Now imagine that cloud of anxiety in the air; start to breathe it in.

4. Just as a plant does with carbon dioxide, your body will metabolize the toxin and you will blow out pure, clean air.

5. Repeat this process and you will eventually "clean up" all the anxiety in the area. You will open your eyes to a calmer, nontoxic environment.

get outside

For anxiety that follows us home and just won't let up, this is the tool we need. Walking through nature is deeply relaxing and quickly alleviates an anxious mood. Research shows that being in nature immediately soothes us and promotes mental health. Also, brain imaging illustrates that nature walks reduce blood flow to the parts of our brain that process anxiety and negative thinking.

So, if you're feeling stuck in an anxious, tense mood, put on your walking shoes and get outside!

visualize

Set aside some quiet time and imagine a positive outcome in detail. Envision the life and experiences on the other side of jealousy, resolution, and relief. Who will be there? What might happen? What will you hear, see, taste, and smell? How will your body feel?

Allow yourself space to really savor the vision of a positive future. The clearer your vision the better.

journal

There have been numerous studies that demonstrate how effective journaling is for health, happiness, and stress management. Plus, it's not only a simple technique but also an enjoyable one. Journaling can relieve stress by helping you work through your anxious feelings. These feelings of anxiety can lead to stress and rumination when left unchecked, but some of the roots of your anxiety can be minimized through a little focused examination. Add a journaling habit to your life, whether you journal daily, weekly, or on an as-needed basis when stress gets to be too intense.

work with your hands

Sometimes, we just need to DO something to release all of our anxious energy. Working on something with our hands is self-soothing because it provides a distraction from our racing thoughts. Repetitive, easy tasks can help distract us from the issue and stop the negative thought cycle.

Here are some things to try:

→ Knitting/crocheting

→ Coloring in a mandala or some other design/image

→ Playing with a fidget spinner

→ Playing an instrument

→ Chopping veggies for a meal

keep a sensory box

Find a special box you like, or just grab any old shoebox. Fill it with soothing objects. Keep it around the house, in your car, or at work. Some people make tiny to-go kits that fit in their bags, too.

Here are a few examples of nice, soothing objects to include:

→ A bottle of fragrant essential oil

→ A bundle of comforting photos (Polaroids are great for this)

→ A favorite book

→ Art supplies

→ Fidget toys or Silly Putty

→ Incense or a candle

practice self-compassion

Be sweet to yourself, and hold yourself accountable with kindness. This means acknowledging mistakes without overidentifying with them (interpreting a simple mistake as a character flaw or taking something too personally) or catastrophizing (exaggerating the situation or assuming the worst outcome). Remember you are learning and growing. You are more resilient than you think, and you will get through this moment.

Create mantras for strength as needed. These might include:

→ "I am stronger than I realize."

→ "I am learning and will do better."

→ "I am not my emotions."

→ "This is short-term. This will pass."

→ "I can handle this."

→ "I will act with integrity."

ACTIVITY

Now let's take note of a few specific ways you can implement these skills when you feel triggered or reactive.

Three self-soothing practices I will try when I am emotionally activated:

Three ways my
partner can support
me when I need
time to practice
self-soothing:

DISCUSSION NOTES

Take time this week to test out these self-soothing techniques,
then discuss them with your partner. Ask each other how you can
best support one another when you're practicing these skills.

stopping distorted thinking

GOALS

→ Identify your distorted thinking patterns.

→ Grow your ability to shift distorted thoughts.

Cognitive distortions are irrational thoughts that have the power to influence how you feel. Everyone has some cognitive distortions—they're a normal part of being human. However, when cognitive distortions are too frequent, rigid, or extreme, they can be harmful.

One common type of cognitive distortion is called catastrophizing. When we catastrophize, we exaggerate the importance of a problem and/or we assume the worst possible outcome to be true.

By learning to question your own thoughts, you can correct many of these cognitive distortions.

TYPES OF COGNITIVE DISTORTIONS

The following are some common types of cognitive distortions.

mind reading

You assume you know what people are thinking without having evidence or proof of their thoughts. *"He thinks I'm an idiot."* *"I'm not going to make the team."*

fortune-telling

You assume you can predict the future—feeling that things will get worse or that there's danger ahead. *"If I go, people will make fun of me."* *"If I talk, I will mess up and not say what I mean."*

catastrophizing

You believe what might happen will be so awful and unbearable that you won't be able to stand it. *"It would be terrible if I failed."* *"If I make a bad grade, I will never get into a good college."*

labeling

You assign general negative traits to yourself and others. *"I'm disgusting."* *"He's horrible."* *"She's irrelevant."*

discounting positives

You claim that the positives that you or others have don't matter. *"That's what I'm supposed to do, so it doesn't count."* *"Those successes were easy, so they don't matter."*

negative filter

You focus almost exclusively on the negatives and seldom notice the positives. *"Look at all the terrible things on the news."* *"Girls never have anything nice to say."*

overgeneralizing

You perceive the likelihood of a negative outcome based upon a single incident. *"I fail all the time." "I'm the worst partner; no one will ever love me." "Online dating just will never work for me"* (after one bad date).

all-or-nothing thinking

You view events or people in all-or-none/black-and-white terms. *"It was a waste of time." "I get rejected by everyone." "Nothing ever goes my way."*

shoulds

You interpret events in terms of how things should be rather than simply focusing on what is. *"I should do well; if I don't, I'm a failure."*

personalizing

You attribute most of the blame to yourself for negative events and fail to see that certain situations are also caused by others. *"My relationship ended because I wasn't fun enough." "It was my fault my group got a bad grade."*

blaming

You focus on the other person as the source of your negative feelings and refuse to take responsibility for changing yourself. *"She's to blame for the way I feel." "My parents caused all my problems." "My teacher is the reason I'm not doing well."*

judgment focus

You view yourself, others, and events in terms of evaluations of "good" and "bad" or "right" and "wrong" rather than simply describing, accepting, or understanding. *"I didn't perform well."*

"I tried it, and I just kept doing it wrong." "Look how successful she is; I'm not that successful."

regret orientation
You focus on the idea that you could have done better in the past rather than on what you can do better now. *"I could have had a better job if I had tried harder." "I shouldn't have said that." "I always mess up."*

what-ifs
You keep asking a series of questions about what if something happens and fail to be satisfied with any of the answers. *"Yeah, but what if I get anxious and I can't catch my breath?"*

emotional reasoning
You let your feelings guide your interpretation of reality. *"I feel sad, therefore I must be depressed." "I feel anxious, therefore I must be in danger."*

inability to disconfirm
You reject any evidence or arguments that might contradict your negative thoughts. *"I'm unlovable. My friends hang out with me only because they must feel sorry for me." "I'm a bad person. I only help others because it makes me feel better about myself."*

unfair comparisons
You interpret events in terms of standards that are unrealistic. *"Others did better than I did on the test." "People my age are more successful than I am."*

ACTIVITY

You may have recognized some of these cognitive distortions in yourself. Think about which distortions might be most common for you and pick one to walk through. You can return to this activity for other distortions on your list individually. Use the following prompts to work through your thoughts.

I am worried that . . .	
How likely is this outcome? Give examples of past experiences or other evidence to support your response.	

If this worry comes true, what's the worst that could happen? Be specific.

If your worry comes true, what is most likely to happen?

What parts of that outcome are within your control?

Is it possible for you to act on any of the items within your control?

Use the following prompts to reality-test your cognitive distortions:

→ If your worry comes true, what are the chances you'll be okay next week? (give a % estimate)

→ If your worry comes true, what are the chances you'll be okay next month? (give a % estimate)

→ If your worry comes true, what are the chances you'll be okay next year? (give a % estimate)

managing tough emotions with discernment

GOALS

→ Identify conversation goals.

→ Increase ability to focus challenging conversations for positive outcome.

→ Initiate tense or tender conversations without igniting defensiveness in a partner.

Often the intense reactions we experience amid jealousy are due to stories we make up ourselves. We fill any gaps in information with assumptions, interpret things, and add our perspective in ways that don't always serve us.

Applying compassionate critical analysis to our internal narratives can help us reclaim some of the power we often lose to jealous reactivity. I like to call this "discernment" because it puts us in position to choose the actions we want to take instead of letting our reactive emotions take control.

ACTIVITY

It can be helpful to write your thoughts out instead of letting them spin in your head. Putting thoughts on paper can take some of their power away.

Think of a time when you felt strong reactive emotions. Describe the story and include assumptions you believed then.

Example: *My partner must have a crush on his new coworker. I bet they have a lot of inside jokes and she's really funny and he looks forward to seeing her every day. I wonder if he thinks she's more attractive than me. He's probably going to leave me one day for someone brilliant like her.*

Using your story, break down your fears into the following categories.

	EXAMPLE	YOUR STORY
VALID	*I wish I knew more about _____like her.*	
INVALID	*He's probably going to leave me one day for someone brilliant like her.*	
NOT SURE	*I wonder if he thinks she's more attractive than me.*	
TRUE	*I bet they have a lot of inside jokes and she's really funny and he really looks forward to seeing her every day.*	
UNTRUE	*He probably doesn't like me anymore because he likes her so much.*	
NOT SURE	*My partner must have a crush on his new coworker.*	

	EXAMPLE	YOUR STORY
LOGICAL	*I bet they have a lot of inside jokes and she's really funny and he really looks forward to seeing her every day.*	
ILLOGICAL	*My partner must have a crush on his new coworker. I wonder if he thinks she's more attractive than me. He's probably going to leave me one day for someone brilliant like her.*	

Now that you have more clarity about the kinds of stories you create in a relationship, let's understand where you have the ability to create change. Our worries, fears, and concerns generally fall into three categories: things we can control, things we can influence, and things we can't control. Use the wheel below to note where your stories fall within these categories.

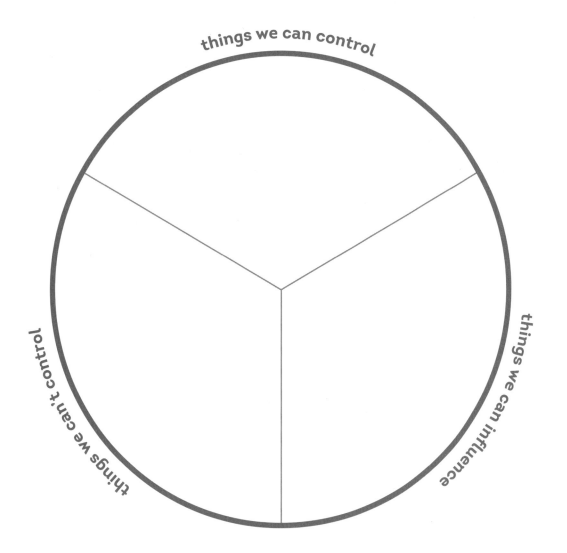

DISCUSSION NOTES

Considering how you completed the wheel above, reflect on the questions below:

→   Which area do most of your concerns or stories fall into?

→   How can you influence these issues in constructive ways?

→   Are there any concerns outside of your control you'd like to let go of?

→   Are your fears telling you the truth?

→   Are there any fears or concerns that you can act on?

2

......

TALKING

THERE ARE moments in our relationships when talking to our partners flows naturally and easily, and there are moments when communication is stifled. We all face moments when we feel stuck in conflict and it gets hard to really understand our partners. In this chapter, we'll work on fine-tuning the skills needed to create space for vulnerability, meaningful support, and authenticity.

creating a secure space *for vulnerability*

GOALS

→ Practice creating safety to share vulnerable moments.

→ Name and share a moment of vulnerability from your past.

→ Identify factors of safety for you and your partner.

Vulnerability is essential to building intimacy and closeness. Vulnerability means risk and emotional exposure and owning something meaningful in the presence of another. Most of us avoid it, numb it out, or try to ignore it, but all of us struggle with it in some aspect of our lives. Couples who manage vulnerability effectively move through conflict with less disruption.

FACTORS THAT CREATE SECURITY

To create a safe spot for vulnerability, we must look at the factors that create security in vulnerable situations:

→ **BOUNDARIES:** Making our commitments to one another clear and trusting we'll respect each other's limits

→ **WARMTH:** Engaging each other with an air of generosity and giving each other the benefit of the doubt

→ **NONJUDGMENT:** Operating from a collaborative mindset instead of right and wrong

→ **INTEGRITY:** Defining our values and aligning our actions with them

→ **SAFETY:** Understanding our unique relationship trauma histories and their impact on our current relationship needs

→ **RELIABILITY AND ACCOUNTABILITY:** Following through on our promises to one another and having space to own our mistakes and repair damage from them as needed

ACTIVITY

Think of two situations: one where vulnerability was handled well and one where it did not go well.

A.

Describe an experience where vulnerability with others went well.

B.

Describe an experience where vulnerability with others did not go well.

Considering situations A and B on the previous page, using the following questions to reflect on and delve deeper into security factors.

when vulnerability went well

→ **SAFETY:** How do you feel safety in your body? What behaviors did the other party reinforce that caused that feeling?

→ **BOUNDARIES:** How had you and the other party established clear commitments and limits with each other?

→ **WARMTH:** How did you demonstrate kindness and generosity with each other?

→ **NONJUDGMENT:** How did you and the other party maintain a judgment-free space with each other?

→ **RELIABILITY AND ACCOUNTABILITY:** What were your accountability practices? How did you and the other party own your mistakes and follow up with each other when harm had been done?

→ **INTEGRITY:** Which of your values were at play in this situation? What helped you act in alignment with those core values?

when vulnerability went poorly

→ **SAFETY:** How did your prior relationship history inform your behaviors and interpretations in this scenario?

→ **BOUNDARIES:** What could you have done to clarify your own boundaries, commitments, and/or limits? How could you have asked for more clarity of the other party?

→ **WARMTH:** Where could either of you have offered the other the benefit of the doubt?

→ **NONJUDGMENT:** Where did you notice judgment (right/wrong, good/bad, too much/not enough)?

→ **RELIABILITY AND ACCOUNTABILITY:** How did you contribute to the problem? How could you hold yourself accountable in the future? What would repair look like in this scenario?

→ **INTEGRITY:** Which of your values were at play in this situation? How were you in alignment or out of alignment with them?

DISCUSSION NOTES

The questions below can help you and your partner reflect on the ways vulnerability and safety contribute to the communication struggles between you. You can write your answers out or discuss them aloud.

→ How can you draw from the factors that increase security in your other relationships to bolster it in this partnership?

→ How can your partner demonstrate warmth as you work through this workbook?

→ What does safety look like while the two of you get vulnerable working through this workbook?

moving from judgment to curiosity

GOALS

→ Identify the judgments present in your partnership.

→ Build your ability to identify the needs underneath surface-level judgments.

Judgment separates us from the people we want to be close to very quickly. Whether it's self-judgment that shuts down opportunity for connection or our judgment of others that makes it hard for loved ones to open up to us, judgment is a killer of authenticity in relationships.

FORMS OF JUDGEMENT

The following are the four most common forms of judgment that show up in relationships:

MORALITY (GOOD/BAD): using a set of principles to distinguish good conduct from bad.

- ➜ "Sugar is bad for you."
- ➜ "If he were a good guy, he would . . ."
- ➜ "My way is just better."

ETHICS (RIGHT/WRONG): using values to establish right and wrong behaviors.

- ➜ "Let me show you the right way . . ."
- ➜ "The truth is . . ."
- ➜ "You're wrong."

MEASUREMENT (TOO MUCH/NOT ENOUGH): using amounts to evaluate worth.

- ➜ "You're being too sensitive."
- ➜ "If you loved me, you would . . ."
- ➜ "This isn't that big of a deal."

COMPARISON: measuring what is against an ideal.

- ➜ "None of my other partners had a problem with this."
- ➜ "Well, all my friends agree with me."
- ➜ "Why can't you be more like . . ."

ACTIVITY

In the space below, list your thoughts without editing until you feel they are complete. Be as honest as you can. Do not share your unfiltered judgments or thoughts with your partner.

Then note the corresponding feeling (or feelings) for each thought. Use the Feelings list in the Appendix (page 232) if you need ideas. You may notice more than one feeling shows up repeatedly; that's fine. Or you may notice additional thoughts show up when you fill in your feelings; that's okay.

	EXAMPLE	YOUR STORY
THOUGHTS	*You're being inconsiderate.* *This relationship is beyond repair.* *You probably deserve better.*	
FEELINGS	*Angry, frustrated, hopeless* *Hopeless, sad, lonely* *Ashamed, embarrassed, guilty, sad*	

DISCUSSION NOTES

Sometimes judgment is a sign that we need to clarify boundaries or accountability processes. What do your thoughts and feelings tell you about your need for boundaries?

Sometimes judgment is a sign that we need to ask for support in an area of life. What do your reflections above tell you about the kind of support you need? What would meaningful support look like for you in this situation?

practicing gratitude to deepen emotional intimacy

GOALS

→ Learn the recipe for emotional intimacy and apply it in your relationships.

→ Deepen emotional intimacy with a shared daily gratitude practice.

Emotional intimacy is something we all deeply crave in relationships. It's the feeling that you're really understood and loved by another not in spite of but along with your imperfections. It's a deep sense of knowing, feeling that someone who really matters to you "gets you." It's arguably the best part of being in a relationship. And it's extremely rare.

INGREDIENTS OF EMOTIONAL INTIMACY

So, how do you practice gratitude and deepen emotional intimacy? There's a recipe you can follow. The ingredients are:

personal

→ State your opinion, interpretation, or thought.

→ Name your personal values and feelings.

→ Use "I" statements.

For example, instead of the statement, "People are always happier during the holidays," these would be more personal:

→ "I am always happier when my travel is booked for the season."

→ "I feel all warm and fuzzy packing my bags for holiday travel."

→ "I'm a big fan of New Year's Eve celebrations."

→ "Hearing this song makes my heart swell."

specific

→ Identify and name observations.

→ Clarify how observations, thoughts, or behaviors are unique to this interaction.

→ Name the other parties involved, and share with them directly.

Examples of specific statements:

→ "I'm always happier in December, and I feel welcome in your house."

→ "Tim and John throw my favorite New Year's Eve party every year."

→ "I really love having all of our family members around one table like this. I miss you when you're not here."

→ "I'm having so much fun right now, I'm already daydreaming about next season."

meaningful

→ Share the interpretation or story attached to your observations.

→ Claim why certain things are important to you.

→ Offer a memory attached to your statement.

→ Share gratitude and appreciation directly.

Examples of meaningful statements:

→ "I really love ugly holiday sweaters. They remind me of my dad when I was growing up."

→ "I'm looking forward to making my grandma's traditional Christmas cookies this year. I really miss cooking with her."

→ "I'm so excited to participate in this year's holiday fundraiser. Service is one of my core values."

present

→ Talk about what you are thinking, feeling, and observing right now.

→ Remember the things that form the past, but tie them to things happening right now.

→ Forecast about the future, but relate your thoughts to things happening right now.

Examples of statements that are more present:

→ "Your joke just now reminded me of the way my sister laughs. I love being reminded of her humor."

→ "Watching the snow fall like this makes me look forward to sledding with our kids this year."

→ "I really love having all of our family members around one table like this. I miss you when you're not here."

ACTIVITY

Set aside 10 minutes every day and use the prompts below to share an emotionally intimate gratitude practice with your partner.

Of the many things you have to feel grateful for and appreciate about your partner, choose one for the duration of this exercise. Take a moment to close your eyes and reflect on the feelings that come up when you think about your partner in this way.

→ What emotions arise?

→ How does this kind of appreciation feel in your body?

→ What do your reflections mean to you?

Once you've taken a few minutes to reflect, share your reflection with your partner using the script below.

PARTNER A: "Of the many things I appreciate about you, one that stands out to me right now is . . ."

PARTNER B: "Of the many things you appreciate about me, one that stands out to you right now is . . ."

PARTNER A: "When I picture you doing (what I said above), I see . . ."

PARTNER B: "When you picture me doing (what you said above), you see . . ."

PARTNER A: "When I think about (what I said above), I feel . . ."

PARTNER B: "When you think about (what you said above), you feel . . ."

PARTNER A: "What (what I said above) means to me is . . ."

PARTNER B: "What (what you said above) means to you is . . ."

When one of you finishes leading all of the prompts in this script, switch roles.

If you enjoy this kind of reflection practice, you may want to deepen your experience by trying Imago Relationship Therapy with a trained professional.

DISCUSSION NOTES

Challenge yourself to track one of the four ingredients of intimacy for the next three days. Notice areas where you could tune up your attentiveness to them, and challenge yourself to be more specific, direct, or present, or to add meaning in your interactions. What shifts when you add intimacy in this way?

recognizing unresolvable conflicts

GOALS

→ Identify your unresolvable issues.

→ Learn to name the unresolvable issues when they arise.

→ Increase compassion by growing awareness and acceptance of these unique issues.

Every couple has a handful of unresolvable issues, but couples who learn to recognize those, accept their differences, and still work through them fare better long-term. These conflicts are often about issues like punctuality, proactivity, schedule management, and spending vs. saving.

ACTIVITY

You and your partner are probably aware of your own unique unresolvable conflicts—the ones you keep arriving at. Name three to five of your most predictable conflict topics.

Once you've named them, consider the following questions:

→ What shifts if you acknowledge you may never see eye to eye on these topics?

→ How could you work together to manage your different philosophies or ways of being without trying to change each other?

These may still be areas of conflict, but accepting that you may always approach them differently is one path to minimizing conflictual conversations.

Now to work through these areas of potential conflict, let's begin with a clear set of intentions. Ask yourself the following reflection questions to clarify your intentions, goals, and boundaries before starting the conversation with your partner.

What is my intention in talking about this topic? How will this conversation help me? Why do I want this conversation to happen?

What needs am I trying to meet by talking about this topic? What feelings am I trying to address?

Am I in a position to truly take my partner's emotions into consideration? Can I really hear them—even if their thoughts and feelings differ from my own?

What does a successful outcome look like here? How do I want to feel at the end of this conversation? How do I hope my partner feels?

How will I take care of the emotions that show up for me if this conversation becomes a conflict? What boundaries need to be in place for me to feel safe? Where can I get support if we need to take space to consider this issue separately?

DISCUSSION NOTES

Next time you notice one of these unresolvable conflict topics come up, ask yourself the questions in the preceding activity before you bring it up to your partner. Notice what shifts when you have a clarified intention at the start of the conversation.

giving the benefit of the doubt

GOALS

→ Develop skills to shift mindset.

→ Increase ability to initiate difficult conversations with warmth.

Trustworthy relationships are built on a foundation of goodwill. Couples with solid trust are able to give each other the benefit of the doubt in conflict, and they weather conflicts more easily because of it.

It's easy to see how more understanding leads us to increased empathy, the ability to take on each other's perspective, and the willingness to collaborate.

Generosity of spirit is an inside job. It's about choosing trust over insecurity or resentment. It's not easy—and it's not for all of our relationships. There absolutely are people who haven't been safe for us to extend our generosity. Use discernment: Who has earned the right to receive your trust?

ACTIVITY

One morning, my partner was a little short with me. He woke up and said, "Get up and help me with the kids." I could've launched into defensive thoughts like, "Why are you being a jerk?"

But I know myself well enough to realize I am less likely to be generous in the morning, so I gave it a minute. Then it hit me: I forgot today was his first day at a new job. He was worried he would be late. With this more empathetic interpretation, my thoughts shifted to "He probably needs extra help today. I would be nervous about getting out the door on time if I were him."

Begin noticing when and where you make less than generous assumptions about your partner. Pick one specific incident. Describe it below:

List five more generous assumptions you could make instead.

Example: *"Maybe he's nervous about this conversation topic."* *"He must not know how important it is for me that he hear this."*

Practicing the skill of turning negative interpretations into positive ones will help you create more space for curiosity and possibility in conflicts moving forward.

DISCUSSION NOTES

Use the following reflection questions to help you shift a difficult conversation.

→ What would be different if you trusted that your partner had nothing but the best intentions?

→ What changes if you allow yourself to believe they're doing the best they can?

LISTENING

NO MATTER HOW much you practice other communication skills, you won't get far without a solid foundation in basic listening skills. Use the activities in this chapter to build a stronger foundation as a listener.

establishing emotional consent

GOALS

→ Begin to understand consent in emotionally intimate moments.

→ Practice ways to respect emotionally intimate moments.

→ Learn tools to establish healthy emotional boundaries.

So many clients come into my office frustrated because no matter how many ways they try to show their partner they're listening and giving support, they seem to miss the mark. One will say they feel unsupported while the other says they give 110 percent support the best they can.

"I just want you to listen," one partner will say.

"All I do is listen," the other replies.

There are a lot of ways to ask for and show support in a partnership. But when we're not clear what kind of support we're looking for and when we don't ask what our partner needs before offering, we're likely to misfire.

I call this *establishing emotional consent*. I ask my clients to check for consent before engaging in emotional vulnerability.

Without clear emotional consent practices, we often misunderstand when listening to a partner and miss the mark when offering support.

ACTIVITY

For this exercise, we will delve into establishing emotional consent with your partner and then gaining clarity around a topic.

First, you should get consent before you initiate or start the conversation. Then you can get more clarity as you share thoughts with your partner. You can also make clarifying statements as you are listening to your partner.

initiating

Stating your intention when you begin (or initiate) the conversation with your partner is one way to establish emotional consent. Here are some examples:

➜ I need some empathy/validation/problem solving/ affection. Do you have time today to talk about _____?

➜ When would be a good time for us to talk about _____?

➜ I want more _____ in my life. Can you help me figure out how to make that happen?

Share one way you could apply this in your relationship:

sharing

Sometimes you don't have a clear intention or request for your partner's action, but you do want to share information. Here are a couple ways to be clear with your partner:

→ I just want to vent and feel heard. Can you just listen to me and paraphrase back what I'm saying?

→ I'm nervous to share this because I don't want _____ and I do want _____. Can you support me by _____?

→ I know I need more _____.

→ When _____ happens, I feel _____.

→ I know I contribute to the problem by _____ _____.

Share one way you could apply this in your relationship:

listening & summarizing

When I am on the listening end of the conversation, it's just as important that I clarify what my partner is seeking when they start a conversation with me. Here are some examples of ways you might try clarifying as a listener:

→ Are you looking for empathy or problem solving?

→ I want to make sure I heard you. Can I repeat what I'm hearing?

→ What I think you're saying is _____ Did I get that right?

→ I understand you're feeling _____ Is there more?

→ How can I support you with this today?

→ Can you repeat that part again? I want to make sure I got it all.

→ Is there more you want to add?

Share one way you could apply this in your relationship:

DISCUSSION NOTES

Think about a conversation you'd like to initiate with your partner. Ask yourself what you're hoping to get from them when you bring up this topic. There's nothing wrong with wanting support from your sweetie, but you're so much more likely to get what you want when you ask clearly. If you need ideas for kinds of support, check out the Needs list in the Appendix (page 233).

building emotional literacy

GOALS

→ Practice naming your emotions.

→ Integrate one simple way to clarify emotions.

→ Get to know your partner better.

One of the most vulnerable things we can do with someone we care about is really tell them how we feel. When we reach out with vulnerability and we receive each other with warmth and caring, we deepen emotional intimacy and grow trust.

However, we can't effectively move through emotional experiences without emotional literacy—it's a prerequisite for empathy and psychological resilience.

As important as it is, most of us need tools to build our emotional vocabulary. We're just not taught this stuff in school. If we want to really build closeness with our partners, it's going to take practice now.

ACTIVITY

1. With the scissors, cut the paper into 40 small pieces.

2. Using the Feelings list in the Appendix (page 232), choose 10 from each category: angry, sad, joyful, and afraid. Write each of those emotions on a piece of cut paper. Put all the pieces of paper in a bowl or jar.

3. Have each person pull a slip of paper without sharing what emotion is on it.

4. Take a moment to think of a time when you felt the emotion you picked. Get a very clear picture in your head. Where were you? Who were you with? What were you doing? How did your body feel? Repeat for the other partner.

5. Share the story of that memory with your partner without naming the emotion you picked. Have them guess which emotion you picked.

6. Don't be disheartened if neither of you guess correctly right away. Instead, use this as an opportunity to reflect and notice how you experience different emotions. There's no right way to feel an emotion; you're simply using this game to share stories and practice guessing emotions without judgment.

DISCUSSION NOTES

If you want to increase your emotional vocabulary, here's a simple practice you can try. Begin each day this week by choosing an emotion from the Feelings list (page 232) at random. Challenge yourself to notice places where that emotion shows up in you or others throughout the day.

developing empathetic communication skills

GOALS

→ Understand the importance of demonstrating empathy in partnerships.

→ Practice taking each other's perspective.

→ Practice validating without judging.

→ Connect more deeply with each other's emotional experience.

Empathy means giving compassionate attention to another by either silently or verbally reflecting their feelings and needs. There's no need to fix the other person's experience, only to offer warmth, acceptance, and respect.

Empathy often requires the ability to be comfortable with uncomfortable emotions. It can be really challenging to stay present for your partner's experience without blaming yourself for their feelings.

Empathetic communication has three critical parts:

→ Emotional connection—deeply connecting with the emotional experience of the other person

→ Perspective taking—working to see things from your partner's perspective

→ Experience validation—validating the other person's experience without judgment

ACTIVITY

Your ability to offer empathy increases when you trust you'll be true to your own feelings and needs. That is, giving empathy to another doesn't mean you're abandoning yourself. Offering empathy doesn't mean you agree, only that you want to understand.

To dive deeper into understanding your feelings and needs, think of three recent occasions: one where you felt nervous, another where you felt happy, and lastly, one where you felt sad. Respond to the questions below.

When was the last time you felt nervous? Where were you? Who was with you? What did you want to happen? How did you feel in your body? What was meaningful or important about that experience?

When was the
last time you felt
happy? Where were
you? Who was with
you? What did you
want to happen?
How did you feel in
your body? What
was meaningful or
important about
that experience?

When was the last
time you felt sad?
Where were you?
Who was with
you? What did you
want to happen?
How did you feel in
your body? What
was meaningful or
important about
that experience?

Take turns sharing the stories for each emotion with your partner. When you're the partner in the listening role, practice demonstrating empathy by responding using only the following prompts:

→ I imagine you were feeling . . .

→ It sounds like _____ really mattered to you.

→ I can see how you would feel that way because . . .

→ It makes sense you would think/feel_____.

→ That must have felt . . .

DISCUSSION NOTES

You can begin to practice your empathetic listening skills with one easy step each day. Challenge yourself to focus on one person in your life once per day. Imagine them in a moment during the day, and guess how they might have felt in the situation.

If you feel comfortable, share with them what you imagined. "I was thinking about what you said in the meeting yesterday. I wondered if you were feeling_____?" or "I was thinking about our conversation yesterday. I wondered if you felt _____?"

Allow them to add nuance to the emotions they experienced, and practice listening to learn more about the different ways the people who matter to you experience different emotions.

separating thoughts from feelings

GOALS

→ Learn to identify thoughts and perceptions.

→ Begin a practice of separating thoughts from feelings.

Our thoughts include the ideas, opinions, beliefs, and attitudes we have about ourselves and the world around us. These thoughts influence how we interpret our experiences, for better or worse. These interpretations are our perceptions, or what we think is happening.

In relationships, it's important to recognize that our perceptions of our partners (while sometimes valid) are not our feelings—and it's important to separate the two. In the following exercise, you'll learn to recognize which words convey perceptions and which ones convey feelings. It will help you develop a strong emotional vocabulary so that you can communicate your personal needs, ultimately creating a strong foundation for couples work.

ACTIVITY

In the following table, create a list of observations that might inform each perception. Then, consult the Feelings list on page 232 and next to each of these perceptions, list one or two possible emotions that you might feel based on this perception.

The point of this exercise is to begin separating our observations, perceptions, and feelings so we can better share them with a partner.

OBSERVATION	PERCEPTION	FEELING
Example: I saw you smile talking to someone else.	Betrayed	Insecure
	Attacked	
	Betrayed	
	Criticized	
	Dismissed	
	Disrespected	
	Invalidated	
	Judged	
	Left Out	

OBSERVATION	PERCEPTION	FEELING
	Manipulated	
	Neglected	
	Patronized	
	Pressured	
	Rejected	
	Smothered	
	Unappreciated	
	Used	

DISCUSSION NOTES

Practice separating your thoughts, perceptions, or interpretations from your feelings by naming them out loud. Try the phrases below to see which of them best help you get clear:

→ "If I try to interpret this, I'd think . . ."

→ "I'm putting that together to mean . . ."

→ "I'm making up a story that . . ."

following up

GOALS

→ Practice asking follow-up questions for a deeper conversation.

→ Use follow-up questions to improve listening.

Couples who stay curious about each other, engage in learning about each other, and are open to growing together fare better long-term. They're able to adapt to changes and navigate bumps in the road with resilience. They also maintain passion and intimacy.

Often, couples are deeply connected (fascinated, really) with each other in the first weeks of the relationship; but as years pass, we build familiarity (which is a good thing), and our curiosity wanes.

We get out of practice staying curiously engaged. Asking strong follow-up questions is one place we can start in an effort to rekindle curiosity.

ACTIVITY

What exactly are strong follow-up questions? For example, if your partner brings up their sister, some potential follow-up questions could be:

→ "If you could change anything about your relationship with her, what would you shift?"

→ "How are you like her, and how are you different from her?"

Think of follow-up questions that ask for more details or go beyond the surface. You can also use simple statements to ask for more. Try sharing your intention like these examples:

→ "Fill me in. I want all the details."

→ "Okay, now I'm curious. Can you say more?"

→ "I want to hear the story behind that."

Now try your hand at it. Think of a subject matter your partner could bring up (work, parents, siblings, hobbies, etc.) and make a list of potential follow-up questions you could ask.

DISCUSSION NOTES

Plan a date with your partner and practice your follow-up questions. Notice which questions get them talking. Notice when you feel resistant to asking questions. What can you learn from those moments?

4

. . . . .

ACCOUNTABILITY
& REPAIR

ONE OF THE MOST common pitfalls for couples in conflict comes when they get stuck in a blame roadblock. They gridlock pointing fingers and are no longer able to move forward.

The antidote to blame is personal accountability.

shifting from blame to personal accountability

GOALS

→ Identify blame when it comes up in your conflicts.

→ Begin conflicts from a place of accountability instead of blame.

Getting stuck in a blaming mindset is one of the most common ways we sabotage our relationships. Blame is a way of releasing anger and defensiveness that blocks our ability to empathize and connect with the people we love. When you start conversations from a place of blame, it's likely your partner will respond with defensiveness. Lots of couples get stuck blaming and finger-pointing and can feel like there's no way out.

PERSONAL ACCOUNTABILITY

The antidote to blame is personal accountability. Every relationship dynamic is created by both of you. Moving to a mindset of accountability means looking at and owning your contribution to the conflict (however small it may be).

Here are a few examples of how a lack of accountability can sound like criticism and blame:

→ "If you would have listened to me, we wouldn't be in this mess right now."

→ "I can't believe you forgot to call the mechanic. I can't trust you to do anything."

→ "You're making me crazy."

→ "This is all your fault."

If I rewrite the examples above from a place of personal accountability, they might sound like this:

→ "I wish I would have held fast to my original suggestion. I compromised too quickly. If I hadn't, we wouldn't be in this mess."

→ "I'm super disappointed you didn't follow through. Can I trust you to make the call today, or should I do it?"

→ "I'm overwhelmed. I need a break from this conversation."

→ "I'm realizing I do things I don't want to sometimes to take care of you. You don't need that. I'm going to take a step back."

→ "I can share some of the blame here. And I want you to take some responsibility too."

ACTIVITY

If you're not asking yourself how you've contributed to the conflicts between you and your partner, you're not being brave enough in conversations—or with yourself.

While many of us struggle with taking too much ownership over things that are not ours, there's always a truth that both parties contribute to every conflict.

Sometimes your part might be as simple as not speaking up or not staying curious; other times it might be a bigger issue, like a tendency to blame or shout, a lack of accountability, an inability to respect boundaries, or projecting insecurities.

Consider a recent conflict with your partner. Identify your blaming mindset and then list three ways you contributed (i.e., personal accountability) to the issue you struggled with.

Blaming mindset

Example: *My partner doesn't care enough about our home to keep up with their half of the chores.*

Personal
accountability

Example: *My partner
isn't doing what
I think is half of
the chores. I could
probably talk to
them to clarify which
things I need more
support on.*

DISCUSSION NOTES

We often overcorrect by shaming and blaming ourselves or
undercorrect by avoiding ways to face accountability directly.

Adding compassion to the accountability process will decrease
shame and isolation and increase growth and connection. Using
self-compassion doesn't mean letting yourself off the hook for
missteps; rather, it means owning them and still holding space
to love yourself. Reflect on the following question:

→   How can I more compassionately hold myself accountable?

understanding your conflict dance

GOALS

→ Identify conversation goals.

→ Increase ability to focus challenging conversations for positive outcome.

→ Learn to initiate tense or tender conversations without igniting defensiveness in a partner.

Couples often get caught in negative or repeating patterns of negative behaviors, thoughts, and feelings that cause distress. You react to your partner's reactions and vice versa, going around and around in a never-ending cycle.

It can feel like a choreographed conflict dance. But once you can understand the moves in your pattern in detail, you can more easily interrupt and change them. Untangling your negative cycle is the first step in climbing out of distress.

WE'RE NOT GETTING ALONG

Check all the statements that reflect the way you feel or what you do when you and your partner are fighting or not getting along. Then review the list, and circle the most important items.

WHAT I DO

- ☐ I chase.
- ☐ I avoid conflict.
- ☐ I become cold or aloof.
- ☐ I check out.
- ☐ I blame.
- ☐ I clam up.
- ☐ I criticize.
- ☐ I defend.
- ☐ I get quiet.
- ☐ I get loud.
- ☐ I escape.
- ☐ I use sarcasm.
- ☐ I leave.
- ☐ I gossip.
- ☐ I withdraw.
- ☐ I numb my emotions.
- ☐ I make jokes.

MY BODY SENSES

- ☐ I feel pressure in my chest.
- ☐ I feel my pulse race.
- ☐ I feel clammy hands.
- ☐ I feel my stomach drop.
- ☐ I feel a lump in my throat.
- ☐ I feel tightness in my shoulders.

- ☐ I feel heaviness in my chest.
- ☐ I feel hot.
- ☐ I feel cold.
- ☐ I feel light-headed or dizzy.
- ☐ I feel tingly.
- ☐ I feel my stomach get upset.
- ☐ I feel achy.
- ☐ I feel lethargic.
- ☐ I feel numb.
- ☐ I feel tension.

WHAT I FEEL

- ☐ I feel afraid.
- ☐ I feel lonely.
- ☐ I feel angry.
- ☐ I feel blank.
- ☐ I feel sad.
- ☐ I feel empty.
- ☐ I feel frustrated.
- ☐ I feel flooded with emotion.
- ☐ I feel guarded.
- ☐ I feel overwhelmed.
- ☐ I feel nervous.
- ☐ I feel confused.
- ☐ I feel guilty.
- ☐ I feel hopeless.

- ☐ I feel insecure.
- ☐ I feel intimidated.
- ☐ I feel disappointed.
- ☐ I feel annoyed.
- ☐ I feel numb.
- ☐ I feel scared.
- ☐ I feel jealous.
- ☐ I feel worried.

WHAT I THINK

- ☐ I am vulnerable.
- ☐ I'm being blamed.
- ☐ I'm being discounted.
- ☐ I'm being controlled.
- ☐ I've been abandoned.
- ☐ I've been let down.
- ☐ It's always my fault.
- ☐ I'm being invalidated.
- ☐ They're shutting me out.
- ☐ They don't think I'm attractive.
- ☐ I don't matter to them.
- ☐ I'm unwanted here.
- ☐ I'm being judged.
- ☐ I'm being disrespected.
- ☐ I'm unlovable.
- ☐ I'm a screw up.
- ☐ I want to get even.

ACTIVITY

This exercise will help you with understanding your negative cycles. Begin by considering your behaviors on the previous page, then complete the following prompts:

My partner often responds to me by (describe their behaviors) . . .

Example: *My partner won't let things drop. My partner withdraws and won't face things with me.*

When my partner responds this way, I often feel . . .

When I feel this way,
I see myself as . . .

When I feel this way,
I long for or need . . .

When I react the
way I do, I guess
that my partner
feels . . .

Draw out your most common repeating negative cycle like a flow chart (include how you and your partner trigger each other's feelings, thoughts, and behaviors).

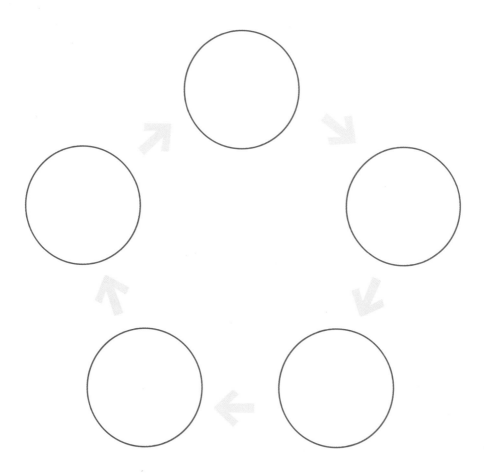

DISCUSSION NOTES

Share your chart with your partner. How are each of your charts similar? Where is there a point you can interrupt these flows?

circling back to repair misunderstanding

GOALS

→ Identify conversation goals.

→ Increase opportunities to turn challenging conversations into positive outcomes.

→ Learn to initiate tense or tender conversations without igniting defensiveness in a partner.

One of the clearest paths to building strong and healthy relationships is practicing mutual, compassionate accountability. This means owning our mistakes and collaboratively moving through them.

To own them, we first need to circle back— after we've had time to process, calm down, or reflect—to important conversations where mistakes were made. In doing so, we need to connect with the person impacted and, without justification, own the ways we've impacted them.

If you feel like you've missed your chance to circle back with your partner, don't worry; there are no time limits to resolving an issue. It can be as simple as saying, "You brought up something important yesterday. Can we try again today?" However, doing it proactively instead of avoiding it or putting it off is far more likely to be a positive experience for both of you.

ACTIVITY

My mentor, researcher Brené Brown, says, "When having difficult conversations, circling back gives us the opportunity to revisit a conversation or interaction after we've had time to fully process. *I need to think about this. Can we circle back in an hour?*"

Sometimes in the middle of a difficult conversation, you find yourself feeling defensive or needing time to think. It can be helpful to request a time-out and circle back to the discussion after a period of time. This signals that you're considering the conversation carefully rather than rushing to placate or dismiss what's being said. *"I think I need a time-out. Can we circle back and finish up this conversation in a couple of hours?"*

Then, write out what you might say to initiate that conversation below.

DISCUSSION NOTES

Considering any mistakes you've noted above, aim to set a time this week to circle back to a conversation with your partner.

making an apology that counts

GOALS

→ Practice creating a healthy apology.

→ Improve conflict-resolution skills.

→ Implement a more complete model for making clear apologies in your partnership.

Apologies in relationships are super important in five critical ways:

1. Solid apologies reinforce the boundaries in relationships. Apologizing lets the hurt party know you do understand what the boundaries are moving forward.

2. An authentic apology can restore dignity to the hurting party.

3. A sincere apology lets the other person know you're not proud of what you've done and you won't be repeating the behavior that caused harm.

4. Accepting responsibility for your actions is an emotionally mature action and can leave you feeling less guilty if you've hurt someone.

5. Apologies are the first step to repairing harm done.

ACTIVITY

Even though apologizing is essential to a healthy relationship, most of us feel so overwhelmed with guilt that we get stuck trying to craft an apology when we need to. It can feel like admitting fault is admitting our flawed character.

In this activity, begin by thinking about actions you've taken that may have caused some annoyance in your partner. Choose one to focus on for this activity.

What was the situation? **Example:** *I yelled at my sweetheart in the car.*	
Ask yourself: What was my hope or intention with the action I took? What was I thinking would happen when I did what I did? **Example:** *I got loud because they never listen to me. I wanted them to stop what they were doing.*	

What were the actions you took in the situation? Think about your tone of voice, physical movements, or words you said.

Example: *I raised my voice and banged my hand on the dashboard.*

What do you think the impact on your partner was?

Example (direct/visible impact): *I could have damaged your car when I hit it.*

Example (indirect/invisible impact): *You probably felt scared or overwhelmed when I did that.*

What would you do differently if you could do things over again? What could you realistically commit to in order to change your future behavior?

Example: *I wish I waited until we got home. I won't bring up tense topics when you're driving again.*

STRONG APOLOGY

How can we structure apologies that bring us closer together without making us feel worse? By answering the previous prompts, you've essentially written all the parts of your apology. A strong apology will follow five steps:

1. **SET ASIDE EXPLANATION AND JUSTIFICATION.** A meaningful apology will focus first on the other party.

2. **NAME AND OWN THE SPECIFIC BEHAVIOR.** Begin your apology by naming the specific actions you took that contributed

continued →

to the problem. It takes two parties to contribute to any conflict, so there will likely be apologies to make on both sides. First focus on your own contributions to the conflict—no matter how small they seem.

3. **NAME AND OWN THE IMPACT ON THE OTHER PARTY.** Specifically address the impact your actions may have had or the impact your partner has already expressed to you. You don't have to agree with their interpretation to acknowledge and validate it.

4. **SUGGEST ALTERNATIVE ACTIONS FOR NEXT TIME.** Tell your partner how you plan to act differently in the future. Be sure you only make promises you can follow through on.

5. **FOLLOW THROUGH ON YOUR SUGGESTION.** Follow-through is where trust is built in relationships, and not doing so is the quickest way to break it. If you can't follow through, you might want to begin this activity over again from step one. Some lack of follow-through is a natural occurrence in any relationship, but too many broken commitments and missing apologies will damage a relationship in time.

DISCUSSION NOTES

Being aware of your default settings for making apologies can inform conflict resolution in the future. Ask yourself the following:

→ Where did I learn about apologies? Who modeled them for me? How was I taught about apologies directly and indirectly?

→ How do the early messages about apologies in my life still show up in conflicts with my partner?

building trust by following through

GOALS

→ Resolve repetitive arguments.

→ Improve conflict-resolution skills.

→ Implement a more complete model for making clear apologies in your partnership.

"Trust is built in the smallest of moments," my mentor, respected relationship researcher John Gottman, says. There are innumerable little opportunities in relationships where we decide either to step toward our partner and build trust or to betray them. Gottman's research has shown that one of the simplest ways our relationships grow distant isn't with one large betrayal, but an accumulation of tiny moments of broken trust over years.

Another important researcher on trust in relationships, Charles Feltman, says that trust is the moment when we choose to make something important to us vulnerable to the actions of someone else. One of the easiest ways to build trust is to reliably show up when our partner needs us. It takes time to build trust because true reliability is built by following through on promises more than once. For example, we need to see changed behavior in the person who harms us more than once to fully trust them.

ACTIVITY

Talk with your partner about the promises you've made to each other. Make a list below of the implicit promises (unspoken but assumed or implied) and the explicit promises (put into words and shared) you've made to each other. List at least 10 for each category below:

Implicit promises

Example: *I will always pick you up at the airport.*

Explicit promises

Example: *I am not sleeping with anybody else.*

Once you've made your lists, take a moment to reflect on your own about the promises you've made and those you've kept.

What do you notice about the times it's been hard to be reliable? Which sorts of agreements are easy to follow through on?

What surprises came up in the conversation with your partner about promises? What did you learn?

Which agreements do you need to make more explicit with your partner?

Which one agreement or promise can you improve your reliability on? What one step can you take this week to improve your reliability?

DISCUSSION NOTES

Consider the places and relationships in your life where you are more reliable. What do you notice about those places? What do they have in common? What can you learn from the differences in your reliability in different contexts? Share what you learn with your partner.

TRUST & INTIMACY

GETTING INTIMACY NEEDS met is one of the key reasons why we build intimate relationships. There are many ways to be intellectually, spiritually, sexually, emotionally, sensually, and functionally intimate with our loved ones; and each friendship or romantic relationship we invest in meets different intimacy needs. Many of us hope to fulfill multiple forms of intimacy needs in one primary relationship. Others look to outsource some of those needs to others. In this chapter, we'll reflect on the different forms of intimacy to identify where you want to build more in your partnership.

building safety for intimacy

GOALS

→ Clarify pathways to safety and security in your partnership.

→ Begin to deepen intimacy in your relationship.

→ Develop increased trust between you and your partner.

Intimacy and vulnerability are so closely linked, it can be hard to tell the difference, so let me explain. Vulnerability is emotional risk or emotional exposure. Being intimate means exposing our vulnerability to another or building closeness and trust.

Before we can increase intimacy in a relationship, we have to feel safe to do so.

ACTIVITY

Find a comfortable place to sit with your partner. Take a few deep breaths together. Begin by thinking about something you appreciate about them. When you're ready, interview your partner using the following questions.

Describe a time you felt safe being vulnerable with a friend. What was it about that friendship that felt safe to you?	
When do you feel most comfortable letting your guard down with other people? What situations make it feel safer to open up?	
Are there any things I can do to make it easier for you to be really open with me? How can I support you when you're being vulnerable?	

Use the space below to reflect on their answers above.

What can you learn from this interview about how you can build safety for intimacy with your partner?

DISCUSSION NOTES

Most of us learn important lessons about intimacy, vulnerability, and safety in our families while growing up. Take 10 minutes to reflect on the ways your family may have directly or indirectly influenced your experience of intimacy.

cultivating physical intimacy

GOALS

→ Clarify your needs for physical and sexual intimacy in your relationship.

→ Begin a conversation with your partner about increasing intimacy between you.

We often overemphasize the importance of sexual intimacy in our lives so much that even the word *sex* is conflated with intimacy. When I ask couples about their sex lives in my office, many of them answer, "We were intimate just last week." They sub in the word *intimacy* for sexual connection. While sexual intimacy is very important, focusing on only one avenue to intimacy leads us to ignore the more complex web of intimacy that makes healthy relationships thrive.

For many people, sensual (or embodied) intimacy and sexual intimacy go hand-in-hand. Think about your current level of fulfillment in and/or desire for embodied intimacy in this partnership. How are those needs being met? Are there ways you'd like to grow this form of intimacy in your relationship?

ACTIVITY

Find a comfortable place to sit with your partner. Take a few deep breaths together. Begin by thinking about something you appreciate about them. When you're ready, interview your partner using the following questions.

How do you most enjoy being invited to sexual intimacy? How do you like me to initiate physical connection with you?

What spaces, situations, or scenarios make it easier for you to let your guard down for sexual connection?

How can we create
an environment
where you'll feel
most physically
safe and secure?
What sort of space
will help you feel
relaxed?

What can I do to
create more safety
or less stress for our
sexual connection?

Use the space below to reflect on your partner's responses.

What can you learn from this interview about how you can build safety for intimacy with your partner?

DISCUSSION NOTES

For some people, sexual and sensual intimacy can be a challenge because they feel disconnected from their sexual or physical selves. To increase sexual or sensual intimacy in your life, spend the day noticing when you feel asexual pleasure and desire. This could be the pleasure of delicious food while eating lunch or the desire for friendship when you're feeling lonely.

Notice when your pleasure and desire arise throughout the day, and challenge yourself to name it using those terms with your partner. Beginning to notice and own your desires and pleasures in asexual contexts will help you begin to notice and honor them in sensual and sexual contexts as well.

emotional, spiritual, & intellectual intimacy

GOALS

→ Identify these forms of intimacy in your own life.

→ Deepen intimacy with your partner by sharing your learning.

Emotional intimacy is often the foundation of deep friendships. It is formed when we are able to be vulnerable with people who gently hold us accountable, can lovingly acknowledge our imperfections, and will reliably show up with warmth.

Spiritual intimacy is sharing awe, inspiration, and revelations with others. For example, this could be discovered in Bible study, a meditation group, yoga practice, a retreat discussion, or on a hike.

The act of learning and sharing knowledge is vulnerable and often deeply connective. This is intellectual intimacy. Some practices include working with a professional coach, attending a writing group, or "geeking out" about a specific topic.

ACTIVITY

Find a comfortable place to sit with your partner. Take a few deep breaths together. Begin by thinking about something you appreciate about them. When you're ready, use the following questions to engage in a conversation with your partner.

What can I do to support you when you're taking an emotional risk?	
Where do you feel most in touch with inspiration or awe? What would help you feel safe to share those moments with me?	
What helps you feel comfortable making mistakes? What does meaningful support look like for you when you are learning?	

Use the space below to reflect on your partner's responses.

What can you learn from this exercise about building the emotional, spiritual, and intellectual forms of intimacy with your partner?

DISCUSSION NOTES

One of the barriers to emotional, spiritual, and intellectual intimacy for most of my clients is they are out of practice experiencing awe, creativity, play, and deep learning. Most of us fail to truly appreciate these special moments in day-to-day life.

To grow your ability to cultivate this sort of intimacy with others, begin by growing your intimacy with yourself. Work to identify the moments of awe and inspiration in your day. When you notice a moment, take a slow breath in and out and pay attention to what awe or inspiration feels like in your body.

Practicing gratitude for both the simple and extraordinary in our daily lives opens up opportunities to share them with loved ones and get closer.

nourishing functional or familial intimacy

GOALS

→ Begin noticing and appreciating familial or functional intimacy in your daily life.

→ Learn to grow functional intimacy as needed in your relationships.

Cohabitating or otherwise building a shared life with a partner often means letting them see your most private and authentic self. Often overlooked, functional intimacy arises as we learn each other's habits of navigating the world around us. Many roommates and families have highly functional intimate lives. They know how the other likes to load the dishwasher, how they prefer to end their day, and what they do to decompress.

Functional intimacy is often the area where greatest trust is cultivated in partnerships. Intertwining finances, logistics, parenting strategies, or holidays can be one of the most meaningful commitments we make in a relationship. However, because it is also usually the least romantic area of a partnership, we overlook it in relationship work. It is less exciting but often far more meaningful in the long-term.

ACTIVITY

Find a comfortable place to sit with your partner. Take a few deep breaths together. Begin by thinking about something you appreciate about them. When you're ready, interview your partner using the following questions.

How can I make your day easier tomorrow? How can I lighten your load in the coming week?

What actions can I take to improve my reliability in the daily function of our shared life? Which tasks, roles, and responsibilities are most meaningful to you?

What helps nourish a feeling of comfort or family for you in relationships?

Use the space below to reflect on your partner's responses.

What can you learn from this interview about how you can increase functional intimacy with your partner?

DISCUSSION NOTES

For most of us, our partner is the most important member of our chosen family. (Our chosen family is not the one we are born into, but the one we gather through friendship and community over our lifetime.) Take a little time to consider what chosen family means in your own life.

Share your reflections with your partner:

→ How are we like a family?

→ How do you define chosen family?

→ In what ways am I most familiar to you? In what ways do I still surprise you?

identifying intimacy needs in relationships

GOALS

→ Identify your needs for intimacy in your relationship.

→ Identify ways to improve intimacy.

→ Talk with your partner about getting your needs for intimacy met.

So many of the issues couples face center around unmet needs for intimacy. Having a clear overview of the different forms of intimacy in your relationship is a useful framework for couples to begin a conversation about it.

In the following activity, you'll consider how each of the six types of intimacy are present in your life, how your needs are being fulfilled, as well as the ways to cultivate more intimacy.

ACTIVITY

Use the diagram below to create a snapshot of this moment in time in your relationship. Add more color or shading to indicate areas where your need is being met more completely right now. Leave blank areas where your current needs could use more attention. Answer the questions that follow to better understand your needs for each form of intimacy.

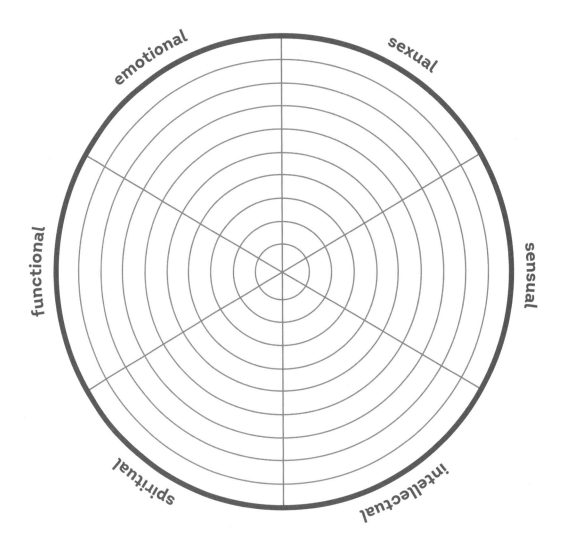

In which areas are you most intimately connected?	
In which areas would you like to increase intimacy in your partnership?	
What behaviors increase intimacy in that area for you?	

DISCUSSION NOTES

Challenge yourself to use the skills we covered in chapters 1 and 2 to begin a conversation with your partner about your needs for intimacy. Notice the specific area of intimacy you'd like to grow, and share a behavior that could help you feel more intimately connected with them.

6

· · · · ·

HEALTHY
BOUNDARIES

BOUNDARIES ARE the walls we put up to protect and guard ourselves from pain, trauma, and chaos. Boundaries are also gateways through which we allow love, energy, and nourishment into our lives. But for most of us, boundaries are a real mystery. Without clear boundaries, it's impossible to build trust with others—or to earn trust from others.

recognizing when boundaries need work

GOALS

→ Identify the signals your body gives you when boundaries need work.

→ Practice listening to your body's signals.

Before we can set clear boundaries, we need to know where they're needed. The good thing is that our bodies and emotions give us signals when boundaries need adjustment. We can usually tell simply by noticing when we feel uncomfortable. Boundary release helps us let go of things that are not serving our health or relationships. The following are types of boundaries we can set:

→ **Protective boundaries** create a barrier to keep out discomfort or harm.

→ **Inclusive boundaries** nourish us by cultivating experiences that help us grow.

→ **Requests and invitations** are boundaries that draw in resources, experiences, or relationships that build us up.

→ **Balancing and filtering boundaries** make sure we establish safe limits to keep our relationships in harmony.

ACTIVITY

Think about a recent interaction where you felt somewhat uncomfortable. Reflect on this experience using the questions below.

What told you a boundary might need attention? What was happening? Who were you with?	
How will you know if your boundaries are working the next time you're in a similar situation? What signals tell you your boundaries are serving you?	

DISCUSSION NOTES

Begin noticing the many different applications of boundaries in your daily life. When you notice discomfort, ask yourself the following questions:

→ What am I trying to protect?

→ What do I need more or less of?

→ How will I know when my boundaries are working?

differentiating among wants, needs, & requirements

GOALS

→ Identify and name your needs in your relationship.

→ Clearly separate needs and wants.

→ Begin a practice of identifying and clearly stating your requirements for your relationship.

If you want to get your needs met in your partnership, you have to start by knowing what they are. Most people get confused about what they really want or need, but with a little careful prep work, you can start asking for what you need directly.

Sometimes, speaking the truth feels like we are being unkind, especially when sharing difficult information or feedback. But in reality, dancing around the truth is unkind. When we avoid stating the truth—when we are vague or ambiguous under the guise of being kind—it is often because we are trying to lessen the discomfort for ourselves, not for the other person.

Direct, honest, straightforward communication is kind. Sidestepping the truth doesn't serve a useful purpose for anyone involved.

ACTIVITY

In this exercise, you will identify your requirements, needs, and wants, which is the first step to setting healthy boundaries. Before creating your own lists on the following page, review the sample lists below.

sample list of requirements

→ Openly shares gratitude
→ Engages in healthy conflict
→ Addiction-free
→ Shows physical affection
→ Listens to challenging feedback
→ Sets clear boundaries
→ Balance of giving and receiving
→ Commitment to self-awareness
→ Shares a common vision
→ Proactive in relationship emotional intimacy
→ Respects each other's feelings
→ Listens to what I want to share
→ Plays and laughs with me
→ Respects each other's opinions
→ Romance
→ Demonstrates flexibility
→ Sexual chemistry/passion
→ Healthy mind, body, spirit

sample list of needs/wants

→ Keep agreements/promises
→ Share domestic chores
→ Organized
→ Financially responsible
→ Detail-oriented
→ Neat/clean
→ Physically affectionate
→ Security-minded
→ Proactive about health and wellness
→ Initiates activities
→ Good communication
→ Effective co-parenting
→ Solid team player
→ Law-abiding

Complete the section below with your requirements, needs and wants. These lists will be helpful for use in Communication Skill #28 (page 126) as well.

your relationship requirements	your relationship needs/wants

DISCUSSION NOTES

Which needs, wants, and requirements are easiest for you to stand up for? Which are more challenging? What might make it easier for you to say no when you need to?

asking for what you need

GOALS

→ Identify judgments as barriers to support in your relationship.

→ Clarify your requests.

→ Practice stating needs and making clear requests.

When your relationship is healthy and trust is strong, you can ask for what you need and your partner can ask for what they need. You can talk to each other about how you feel without judgment. Strong couples help and support each other without judgment and with great ease.

Unfortunately, many of us have trouble asking for help and support in our intimate relationships. We fear being vulnerable or looking weak. And yet, being witnessed and supported in our most vulnerable moments is the quickest pathway to building deep connection between people who love each other.

ACTIVITY

Now that you are aware of requirements, wants, and needs
(see your list, page 125), it's to time communicate them to your
partner. Choose three of your wants/needs from your list. Fill in
the following "I" statements to make requests for these needs.

→ "I'm needing more _____ (need).
   I realized when I don't have enough of that I feel
   _____ (feeling).
   Could you _____ (request)?"

→ "I know I was _____ (feeling)
   earlier. I think it's because I need more
   _____ (need).
   It would help me if _____ (request)."

→ "I think I've been short lately because I need more
   _____ (need)
   at _____ (location).
   I'd love it if you could support me by
   _____ (request)."

DISCUSSION NOTES

Make one of the requests or actions you identified in the above
activity. When you envision yourself making this request, note
the responses from your body. What do you feel? What might
those feelings mean?

moving toward, away, & against

GOALS

→ Identify your most common response: moving toward, away, or against.

→ Implement tools to interrupt reactive patterns and replace with intentional choices.

When we find ourselves in need of a boundary adjustment, it's common for our defenses to show up in the form of us moving away, toward, or against someone we care about. Moving away can mean withdrawing, silencing ourselves, or keeping secrets in an attempt to avoid discomfort or conflict. When we move toward someone, we are seeking to please and appease, or as a method of avoiding discomfort or conflict. Finally, when moving against, we are trying to gain power over another by being aggressive and controlling. Here, too, our goal is to avoid discomfort or conflict. Although we use these maneuvers in an attempt to self-protect, the ultimate result is disconnection.

ACTIVITY

Find a comfortable place to sit with your partner. Take a few deep breaths together. Begin by thinking about something you appreciate about them. When you're ready, use the questions below to interview your partner. In the space provided, take notes while they answer.

What did your family teach you or model for you about asking for help in relationships?

What can I do to make it easier to move toward me when you need help?

When do you notice me moving away or against you in our relationship?

DISCUSSION NOTES

Build self-awareness this week by tracking your default patterns and habits of moving toward, away from, or against your partner in small actions every day. What common behavior patterns do you notice as you review your week?

using a mindful approach to conflict

GOALS

→ Incorporate mindfulness into your boundary-setting practices.

→ Pay closer attention to your inner cues that your boundaries need work.

Practicing mindfulness can help us build stronger relationships. It's a great technique for calming reactive emotions when they arise. Mindfulness helps us pay attention to the cues our body is giving us. It can also help us distill what we need most in conflicts. With this skill, you'll learn how to mindfully approach difficult conversations.

MINDFULNESS FOR DIFFICULT CONVERSATIONS

A mindful approach can improve your chances of getting your point across in difficult conversations. Before you enter into the conversation, take a review of the purpose, points of view, and potential solutions. Consider these your mindfulness action steps.

1. **IDENTIFY THE PURPOSE OF THE CONVERSATION.** Being clear about your purpose will help you get what you need from the conversation. Write out your hopes and intentions in bringing it up.

2. **ASK YOURSELF, "WHAT IS MY SIDE OF THE STORY?"** Think about what the story means to you. When expressing your story, start your sentences with "I" statements, such as "I feel bad about the way our evening ended last night."

3. **LIST THE FEELINGS THE SITUATION INVOKES.** Identifying your feelings will help your partner connect with your experience in a more powerful way.

4. **IMAGINE YOUR PARTNER'S SIDE OF THE STORY.** Work to put yourself in their shoes.

5. **IMAGINE HOW YOUR PARTNER IS FEELING.** What emotions might the situation be eliciting in them? Challenge yourself to find compassion for their emotions.

6. **CONSIDER WHERE YOU CAN COME TOGETHER.** What is your common ground? What solution might meet both of your needs?

7. **VIEW THE SITUATION WITH AN OPEN (BEGINNER'S) MIND.** This means approaching from a place of openness and curiosity. Even if this is a conversation you have had many times, there may be new information.

After going through these steps, you may realize that you no longer need to have the conversation. If you decide to move forward with the discussion, you'll be able to enter with a more empathetic and understanding perspective. But before you begin, be sure to start with mindful breathing and take a few deep diaphragmatic breaths. Scan your body for tension. Breathe into these areas to release tension, then enter into the conversation.

ACTIVITY

Try to use this mindful approach for any difficult conversations that come up over the week. As you try these mindfulness actions, give yourself a rating of 1 to 5 (1 needs work, 5 is very success-ful) that represents how well you're adhering to the steps. Notice which action steps flow more freely and which come less easily.

The steps that come easier to you may already be a part of your "default settings." That means you can work on the steps that feel less familiar to you.

DISCUSSION NOTES

Part of recognizing our default settings is identifying the tools and skills we don't often choose and working to improve confidence in those areas. Push yourself to move beyond your comfort zone, and try implementing a tool or skill you don't typically use as a default. Ask yourself:

→ Which tools do I rely on most heavily?

→ How could I challenge myself to practice one of these in the coming week?

part two

• • • • • •

RELATIONSHIP ISSUES

(and how to talk about them)

yes, your relationship is unique, but there are several key conflicts common to most couples. These include sexual intimacy, careers, financial resources, family, friends, and your shared home. Is your top conflict on this list? Most couples struggle with at least one of these during the course of their partnership.

In this section, we'll address the most prevalent issues that lead to communication breakdowns using real-life scenarios from my couples counseling practice. (Note: In order to protect my clients' anonymity—and because these issues come up so frequently—I will be combining stories, changing names, and disguising the specific details of my clients' situations.)

I'll walk you through these common relationship problems and discuss what's happening both from the couple's perspective and from mine as a relationship expert and observer.

Then we'll use the skills that we learned in the previous section to address the communication breakdown that's occurring and open pathways for connection. I'll walk you through guided exercises to support you through similar conversations and conflicts in your own relationship.

7

. . . . .

INTIMACY

SEXUAL ISSUES are one of the most common concerns for couples and are usually the most difficult to talk about. In this chapter, we'll look more closely at the most typical sexual problems couples bring up in my practice and expand on the skills from Part One to address and destigmatize these common relationship issues.

diminished desire

Katie and Kira have a lot going for them. Last year, they moved together to Seattle from Iowa for new careers, and they live in a beautiful downtown condo. They met as sophomores in college and were best friends for two years before Kira told Katie she had feelings for her, and they fell head over heels. Five years later, it seems each of their professional dreams are coming to fruition.

Their friendship has remained strong, but as the stress of the move and work ramped up, Kira's sex drive slowed way down. They thought it might come back once their new routines were established, but it's been a year, and Katie is tired of her flirtatious passes going seemingly unnoticed. Katie's growing impatience has them in therapy for "sexual issues."

WHAT'S GOING ON

It's clear the current arrangement isn't working for Katie. Often the partner in Katie's position can feel guilty about pressuring their partner for sex, and can **feel** extreme rejection if their attempts to connect have been turned down repeatedly. It's also not unusual for the partner in Kira's position to feel over-whelmed, checked out, and/or resentful sexually. When someone is overloaded, sex can begin to feel like just one more obligation to fulfill.

High-stress couples often have the lowest sexual chemistry. The stress of several major life transitions (graduating, moving, starting new jobs) has Kira and Katie experiencing what is a very normal lull in their sexual activity. Every long-term couple will experience ebbs and flows in their sexual connection over the years. Our culture points out that this is a sign of relationship trouble, but that's not entirely true. Even the healthiest, most connected relationships will have more sex sometimes and less sex other times. Don't let a little sexual disconnection throw you.

ADDRESS THE ISSUE

1. Before starting, do a quick scan of both of your physical and mental states. Does one of you feel hungry or tired/exhausted? If yes, address those basic needs first and make an appointment to regroup.

2. Find a quiet space without distractions. It might be good to get outside of your house and go to the park or even talk in the car.

3. Apply Skill #11: Establishing Emotional Consent (page 66) to begin the conversation in a positive direction with clear emotional consent.

4. Practice Skill #16: Shifting from Blame to Personal Accountability (page 83) to move from finger-pointing about your sexual disconnection to taking personal accountability for the ways you've grown distant.

5. Review Skill #2: Identifying Reactivity (page 20) and Skill #3: Learning to Interrupt Reactivity (page 24) to help you reconnect with your individual needs and understand the reactivity that comes up in your conversations.

6. Begin slowly working through Skill #21: Building Safety for Intimacy (page 104); Skill #22: Cultivating Physical Intimacy (page 107); Skill #23: Emotional, Spiritual, & Intellectual Intimacy (page 111); Skill #24: Nourishing Functional or Familial Intimacy (page 114); and Skill #25: Identifying Intimacy Needs in Relationships (page 117) to talk more specifically about your and your partner's needs for intimacy.

TIP   Don't forget to look at the parts of your connection that are strong. You might be able to use those strengths to shift the disconnect in your bedroom.

DISCUSSION NOTES

Everyone has a set of sexual brakes and gas pedals. Coming to some understanding can help increase sexual connection and improve shared sexual experiences.

Identify your sexual brake pedals. They can be anything about your environment, senses, interpretations, or fantasies that slows or stops sexual arousal. Then share these findings with your partner, with the goal of stating your desires rather than placing blame.

no sex

Rhianna and Martel are a highly respected couple in St. Louis. They have two kids, Tasha (6) and Kevin (8), whom they adore, and they describe themselves as a great team. They are the center of their social universe, chairing fundraisers, organizing events, and hosting holiday gatherings for their large network. They are highly affectionate, often holding hands and smiling at each other. Their positive attitudes make them a lot of fun to be around.

They are high-achieving, kindhearted leaders—a truly magnetic couple. People would be shocked to discover that the warmth between them has been stifled by a sexual rut lasting more than three years. Somewhere along the way, their sex life tapered off, and neither Rhianna nor Martel know how to restart things.

The sex they had in the past was highly satisfying, but it seems as though both these incredible people forgot how to have it.

WHAT'S GOING ON

Lots of busy modern couples experience sexual disconnection. It's incredibly common for people to put work, volunteering, grad school, kids, you name it, before sex—sometimes for years. I see it all the time in my practice, and most couples hide it well among peers who think they lead a perfect life. Those false assumptions can leave them feeling isolated when they secretly struggle with something. The other problem is that couples assume their sex life will just come back easily without maintenance, and that's not always true.

Contrary to popular myths, sexual connection requires attention just like any other part of a healthy relationship if it is going to survive the test of time. The busier a couple's lives become, the harder but more important it is that they carve out time to connect sensually and erotically on a regular basis.

ADDRESS THE ISSUE

1. Before starting, do a quick scan of both of your physical and mental states. Does one of you feel hungry or tired/exhausted? If yes, address those basic needs first and make an appointment to regroup.

2. Find a quiet space without distractions. It might be good to get outside of your house and go to the park or even talk in the car. It's easier to address sexual issues outside of a sexual context.

3. Use Skill #2: Identifying Reactivity (page 20) over the course of a week, and pay close attention to your body's subtle ways of telling you you're in the mood or open to affection. Being mindful of your needs may help you take advantage of those moments.

continued →

4. Use Skill #8: Practicing Gratitude to Deepen Emotional Intimacy (page 53) to help you express appreciation based on your past sexual experiences and future fantasies. Reminiscing about positive sexual experiences and fantasizing together outside of sexual activity help most couples reignite fires of attraction. However, it is also important to spend time physically connecting as well— even if it's not having sex. Building in physical affection will also help shift any stuck sexual patterns.

5. Use Skill #4: Stopping Distorted Thinking (page 30) to highlight ways your own thoughts might be getting in the way of your sexual connection. Even the most outwardly positive couple, like Rhianna and Martel, get stuck in these thought patterns internally and need to flush them out once in a while.

TIP Don't be afraid to make a "sex date" or a "make out date" where you reliably make time to prioritize physical connection centered on both partners' pleasure.

DISCUSSION NOTES

It can be difficult for some of us to engage with a sense of real confidence; a core ingredient of sexiness. Even couples who seem to have it all can struggle with this because their high standards will always leave them feeling inadequate.

Spend the week paying attention to the factors that heighten your feeling of sexiness. Once you have a full list, invest energy in feeling sexy using one of these factors every day.

sharing new sexual fantasies

Bree hasn't always been the confident woman you see when you meet her today. While her 38-year-old self is traveling the world reading every self-improvement book she can get her hands on, she was once severely sexually repressed by her religious upbringing. She's done a lot of work to explore her shame and overcome personal limitations, and is finally enjoying the benefits of all that hard work.

She began online dating with the hope she'd have time to explore and enjoy more of this new sexual self. But when Patrick's profile popped up, their chemistry was so instantaneous that she set aside the apps to spend time with him.

In their very first sexual encounter, Bree knew something was different. Patrick was the kind of partner with whom she could feel comfortable being her authentic self, but she was also interested in exploring new pleasures. How could she share them with him without scaring him off?

WHAT'S GOING ON

Lots of people struggle to open up about new sexual fantasies and interests. But discovering new parts of our sexuality is a normal part of life—and such an important one to share with your partner. It's important Bree and Patrick create a judgment-free space to talk about their sexual needs more easily.

It is not at all unusual to expand and shift sexual interests over the course of a lifetime. Make sure you and your sweetheart are making time for sexual play and exploration to keep up-to-date on your desires.

ADDRESS THE ISSUE

1. Before starting, do a quick scan of both of your physical and mental states. Does one of you feel hungry or tired/exhausted? If yes, address those basic needs first and make an appointment to regroup.

2. Find a quiet space without distractions. It might be good to get outside of your house and go to the park or even talk in the car.

3. It's important to lay a clear foundation using Skill #6: Creating a Secure Space for Vulnerability (page 44) and Skill #11: Establishing Emotional Consent (page 66) to clarify your intention and consent for this subject matter. Focus on what will make it easier for you as a couple to feel supported while opening up.

4. Practice Skill #12: Building Emotional Literacy (page 71) and Skill #13: Developing Empathetic Communication Skills (page 73) to help your partner receive and validate your sexual fantasies even if they don't share these same fantasies.

TIPS You don't have to share fantasies to be great partners. One partner may have more curiosity about specific sex acts than the other. You simply want to hold judgment-free space for each other's expression.

It's not uncommon for folks to hold certain fantasies without ever intending to act on them. Get clear about the level of action, conversation, or fantasy play your partner wants to experience before jumping to conclusions about what their desires might mean to you.

DISCUSSION NOTES

You can also apply Skill #29: Moving Toward, Away, & Against (page 128) when you approach conversations about sex. Notice when you move toward, away from, or against your partner related to sexual issues. How or when do those defenses serve you? How or when do they get in your way?

desire fatigue

Adam came into my office feeling pretty impatient. He and Eryka used to have a sex life they were both satisfied with, but that was three years ago. Slowly over time, they stopped getting frisky as often, and their frequency dropped from a couple times a week to monthly and then quarterly. By the time they came to me, Adam felt like they had tried everything, but he and Eryka were never on the same page. He was feeling rejected all the time.

Eryka, fully admitting her libido had dropped a little, said she was having the same experience. Though she was initiating less often, she felt that Adam just wasn't as into it as he had been back in their early days. Every time she perceived him as uninterested, it made her less likely to initiate again, until she'd nearly stopped trying.

WHAT'S GOING ON

Couples who lose passion slowly over time are experiencing what is called *desire fatigue*. While this is a common occurrence, there are simple strategies to help manage these experiences. The most important thing is for couples to have clear, direct, honest, and kind sexual communication. Couples who can name their desires without judgment or pressure to act, practice active consent during sexual acts, and discuss ways to change plans and activities in the middle of the act without ego trouble are well prepared to navigate the changes that are sure to come about in their shared sex life.

The other critical skill set is making sure both partners have a sense of autonomy and strong self-care/stress management skills. Partners who are better equipped at accessing personal agency, confidence, creativity, and relaxation are more likely to tap into their sexual energy.

Know that lots of people really struggle to communicate about sex. Talking about it can feel too risky, vulnerable, or even arousing to do face-to-face. Consider the environment that will be most conducive to your sharing openly and honestly about your sexual experiences and desires.

ADDRESS THE ISSUE

1. Before starting, do a quick scan of both of your physical and mental states. Does one of you feel hungry or tired/exhausted? If yes, address those basic needs first and make an appointment to regroup.

2. Find a quiet space without distractions. It might be good to get outside of your house and go to the park or even talk in the car.

continued →

3. If you and your partner are like Eryka and Adam, begin with Skill #21: Building Safety for Intimacy (page 104) to lay a foundation for your conversation about sexual intimacy. Focus on what will help both of you feel safe and comfortable talking this through.

4. Once you've talked through Skill #21, you can adapt it to focus on what helps both of you feel sexy or confident, relaxed, and open for connection. Creating a clear vision of this environment will help you set the stage in the future for an intimate connection.

TIPS   Many of us fall into a trap of taking sexual issues personally. Do your best to focus on the specific objective behaviors that contribute to the sexual issues between you and your partner, rather than interpreting them as a sign of personal shortcomings (see Skill #14: Separating Thoughts from Feelings, page 77).

Don't worry if it takes lots of practice to feel comfortable talking explicitly about your sexual needs. That is a very common experience. Keep regularly challenging yourself to talk about them with your partner to build skills and self-compassion.

DISCUSSION NOTES

Initiate a conversation about sexual issues this week. Instead of waiting until a sexual moment doesn't go as planned, consider addressing sexual issues when neither one of you is trying to initiate sexual connection. Normalize your sexual conversations just like any other relationship issue so you can work on them when the issue isn't as emotionally loaded.

bad sex

Neko and Kai had been looking forward to their first Bonnaroo Music Festival trip for a year. They saved and planned all the fun they'd have and hoped it would be a magical experience for their relationship.

But their first night in the tent came after a long day of drinking and partying. Kai was really tired from day drinking in the sun, and Neko was feeling disconnected. Kai decided to end the day early and went into the tent. Neko had a few more drinks and went in after him. The details are blurry from a long day and too many beers, but somehow they ended up in a complicated tangle of sex and emotional conversations that neither of them remembers very well.

What they both do remember is a night of bad sex and complicated feelings, and they haven't found a way to work through the issue on their own.

WHAT'S GOING ON

Many couples experience off nights sexually and struggle to talk about them. Creating a safe space to talk about vulnerable sexual experiences is the best way to resolve misunderstandings and confusion. Sexual issues are usually never only about sex. More often, the root issues are communication, safety, intimacy, or self-care boundaries.

ADDRESS THE ISSUE

1. Before starting, do a quick scan of both of your physical and mental states. Does one of you feel hungry or tired/ exhausted? If yes, address those basic needs first and make an appointment to regroup.

2. Find a quiet space without distractions. It might be good to get outside of your house and go to the park or even talk in the car.

3. Use Skill #6: Creating a Secure Space for Vulnerability (page 44) and Skill #21: Building Safety for Intimacy (page 104) to build a safe pathway to communicate about this tender issue.

TIP   According to research, the way you start the conflict is also the way it will likely end. Practicing a compassionate and open-minded start to tense conversations will help you both maintain compassion throughout.

DISCUSSION NOTES

Think of an experience where you felt really well understood by your partner. What were their actions that helped you feel this way?

8

· · · · ·

CAREER

OUR PROFESSIONAL PASSIONS and creative pursuits are some of the greatest joys in our lives. They fill our need for contribution and legacy while supporting our families financially. We will use this chapter to address the common ways our work and career focus can impact intimate relationships.

personal purpose clarity

Sasha has been working full-time her entire adult life. She's met every target and goal she's set for herself and is nearing her 10-year anniversary at her firm. She knows she should feel proud, but more than anything she feels a little bewildered.

"How'd I get here?" she asks in my office. "I feel like I picked a major in college and then was carried through the last fifteen years on an energy flow I never considered. I mean, is this even what I want for my life?"

Sasha's lost sense of self has effects at home as well. Luis, her long-time partner, has noticed her seeming slightly distant and wants more of her full presence on their dates and in the bedroom. But Sasha can't seem to find herself at home either, leaving them both confused, disappointed, and disconnected. Their issues are the worst in the bedroom. Sasha has just lost all interest. And that's what ultimately brought them into couples work with me.

WHAT'S GOING ON

So many couples come into my office frustrated with their partner's lack of presence at home (in the bedroom and beyond). Many of them say even when they spend time together, they never really feel like their partner is with them—they might be on their phone or thinking about work instead of paying attention.

I see lots of couples who experience sexual disconnection as a side effect of stress in their lives. When we're stressed, it's very difficult to experience pleasure and to connect with our body. It's essential to find ways to address the stress both partners feel so they can be more present to each other and to themselves.

And in Sasha's case, the malaise and lack of passion she's feeling at work must be addressed in order to help her tap into a sense of passion at home. Whenever I give talks on pleasure and desire in relationships, I hear from audience members who feel a general lack of desire in their lives and also struggle to connect with sexual desire and passion. Finding pathways to personal desire and passion is a critical first step to reclaiming it at home.

ADDRESS THE ISSUE

1. Before starting, do a quick scan of both of your physical and mental states. Does one of you feel hungry or tired/exhausted? If yes, address those basic needs first and make an appointment to regroup.

2. Find a quiet space without distractions. It might be good to get outside of your house and go to the park or even talk in the car.

3. Start with Skill #21: Building Safety for Intimacy (page 104) to create greater safety between you and your partner to address both of your physical intimacy needs.

continued →

4. Both partners, but especially the person who identifies with Sasha, might want to spend time focusing on Skill #2: Identifying Reactivity (page 20) and Skill #26: Recognizing When Boundaries Need Work (page 121) to really listen to what they need and start creating better boundaries in their home and work life.

TIP   It can be really useful to invest in personal work with a therapist or coach when you're also working on your relationship. Often, one partner's individual stress can cause conflict in the relationship, so having individual support can help move you forward as a couple. In this scenario, Sasha might benefit from support from a mentor, coach, therapist, or career counselor.

DISCUSSION NOTES

It can be really beneficial for couples to discuss their needs and expectations for stress management before it becomes an issue between them. Here are a few questions you may want to ask each other:

→ How will I know when you're starting to get stressed?

→ How can I best support or encourage you in moments of stress?

→ How should I let you know if I'm concerned about your stress level?

→ What can I do to bring greater ease to your week?

career & legacy

When Amanda and Adam started their doggie daycare, it came from a simple love of dogs and a drive to do work that made them smile. They had no idea their simple dreams would grow into a doggie grooming, daycare, and pet-training business with multiple locations in three states.

Though their success has been unmistakable, Adam has started wondering if there's not something more he wants to do with his life, causing Amanda to worry if he's thinking of leaving her or just thinking about leaving the business.

WHAT'S GOING ON

For this couple, their professional accomplishments have become part of their identity. I worked with them to break some of the enmeshment (overidentification) they have with each other and with their work. It's common for couples who work together to have struggles with independent relationships and interests. Make creating space for autonomy and independence a priority so it can become a natural part of your relationship over time.

ADDRESS THE ISSUE

1. Before starting, do a quick scan of both of your physical and mental states. Does one of you feel hungry or tired/exhausted? If yes, address those basic needs first and make an appointment to regroup.

2. Find a quiet space without distractions. It might be good to get outside of your house and go to the park or even talk in the car.

3. Use Skill #12: Building Emotional Literacy (page 71), Skill #14: Separating Thoughts from Feelings (page 77), and Skill #15: Following Up (page 80), to frame your conversation and engage the feelings around changing careers or shifting the way you work together.

DISCUSSION NOTES

Ask your partner:

→ **How can I support your independence?**

→ **What can I do to help you take time for yourself?**

→ **How can I stay connected to you while also supporting your need for autonomy?**

professional purpose

Brandon has always been the funniest guy in the room. Everyone looks to him as the life of the party. He's often hosting and emceeing events for his corporation. Maxwell has loved being the man on his arm for 17 years.

But lately, Brandon's humor has turned a little sharp when they're out. He's been making tiny jabs at Maxwell's career in nonprofits, leading them to exit parties quickly to fight in private. Maxwell is starting to think Brandon doesn't respect his work.

WHAT'S GOING ON

In this specific case, what Brandon may not even realize yet is underneath those jabs there is a sense of insecurity; he has watched his body age while Maxwell only seems to look younger every year. He's starting to worry he'll become unattractive to Maxwell in time.

However, his sarcasm is the only unattractive quality Maxwell sees in Brandon, and it's creating more damage. My goal in our session was to create practices that reassure Brandon of their connection and support him in repairing the damage his humor has done to the relationship.

Ultimately, when we started talking about both men's sense of professional purpose, they shared deep insecurities about their work. Brandon worried his work wasn't leaving the kind of legacy he'd like and envied Maxwell's commitment to their community through his work. Maxwell, on the other hand, shared that he had always felt insecure about the income gap in their relationship. He worried Brandon would resent him when they're old for unequal contribution to their retirement accounts.

Most of us experience complex emotions related to our household income contributions, our legacy, and sense of purpose at work. Our partners often become an easy target for our insecurities. Having open and honest conversations about these topics can help you create understanding instead of miscommunication.

ADDRESS THE ISSUE

1. Before starting, do a quick scan of both of your physical and mental states. Does one of you feel hungry or tired/ exhausted? If yes, address those basic needs first and make an appointment to regroup.

2. Find a quiet space without distractions. It might be good to get outside of your house and go to the park or even talk in the car.

3. Use Skill #13: Developing Empathetic Communication Skills (page 73), Skill #18: Circling Back to Repair Misunderstanding (page 92), and Skill #19: Making an Apology That Counts (page 94) to start apologizing for and repairing hurtful comments.

4. Review Skill #27: Differentiating among Wants, Needs, & Requirements (page 123) and Skill #28: Asking for What You Need (page 126), and reflect on how you might address this issue differently in the future.

TIPS   People sometimes use sarcasm as a way to deflect hurt and insecurity. While that explanation can help you hold compassion for them, it's still okay to ask them to change their behavior. Your hurt is valid even when you have compassion for your partner.

Humor can be an excellent tool to defuse conflict in partnerships, but sarcasm and teasing may only fuel the flames of conflict. Take careful note of which direction your humor is heading with your partner.

DISCUSSION NOTES

Take time this week to reflect on the following questions about work and humor:

→ When or how do you feel insecure about your work, income, or legacy? How can you initiate more conversations about these topics with your partner?

→ How are you proud of your partner's work, legacy, or contribution? Ask them how you might express that pride in ways that feel good to them.

→ Growing up, how was humor used in your family? What did your family of origin teach you about sarcasm, teasing, or jokes when emotions were high?

→ How were your experiences similar to and different from your partner's?

visioning & long-range plans

Since she was a child, Sadie dreamed of a life in the country, rescuing pit bulls and growing her own tomatoes. So, it was really exciting when she met Joelle, who shared her passion for wide-open spaces and rehabilitating four-legged friends.

But when they started looking at properties in eastern Oregon, Joelle got nervous. She knew she wanted that life in the country, but she wasn't quite ready for it yet. Sadie was beyond ready.

Joelle's sudden nervousness left Sadie wondering if she truly shared their vision. It caused Sadie to question other parts of their relationship.

Joelle, on the other hand, started wondering about her own identity. What was holding her back? It called into question so much of what she thought she knew about herself. And while Joelle sorted through these big personal questions, Sadie's need for reassurance intensified her confusion.

They came to me wanting to find a compromise they could live with until they were both ready to move.

WHAT'S GOING ON

It's not unusual for partners to feel shaken when plans change. It's okay if either of you feels nervous when making important life decisions and navigating transitions. Learn to expect nervousness to show up for both of you in different ways when you're making changes. When we expect it as a normal part of the process, we can be more accepting of each other as we work through the issue.

In my work with this couple, I wanted to help them create a new shared vision and identify milestones they could celebrate as they moved forward together. This can work to reestablish trust and a sense of togetherness.

ADDRESS THE ISSUE

1. Before starting, do a quick scan of both of your physical and mental states. Does one of you feel hungry or tired/exhausted? If yes, address those basic needs first and make an appointment to regroup.

2. Find a quiet space without distractions. It might be good to get outside of your house and go to the park or even talk in the car.

3. Immediately start from Skill #1: Building Awareness of Your Defaults (page 13) to better understand your default relationship settings. Understanding your defaults can help you clarify your perspective with your partner and might help you see things through their eyes.

4. After getting clearer about baselines, review Skill #6: Creating a Secure Space for Vulnerability (page 44) and Skill #7: Moving from Judgment to Curiosity (page 49) to help you start a conversation about the changes in your life from a more compassionate place.

TIP Healthy couples adapt to changes in their life. Just because you're experiencing changes in your life doesn't mean your relationship is in a bad place. The ability to navigate challenges with openness, curiosity, and commitment are great signs of growth.

DISCUSSION NOTES

Every couple needs a shared vision they're working toward. This can be going to a concert, dreaming of growing old together, or anything in between. It doesn't have to mean large commitments but does imply an intention to spend time together in the future.

Creating a unified vision helps you feel grounded in your connection, working as a stronger team toward a shared goal. If you don't already have set goals for your partnership, identify some of your shared goals by creating a relationship bucket list of adventures or experiences. This might include travel, studies, experiences, or life milestones you can begin working on or planning together.

transparency, honesty, & trust

*"I don't know why, but Laurie just doesn't like him,"
Xia tells me in our very first session. "Chris has done
everything in his power to impress her, but she's
always been cold." The tension between Xia's best
friend, Laurie, and Xia's boyfriend, Chris, has grown
beyond a cool demeanor to a frozen stalemate.*

*Xia feels torn between her longest friendship and
her relationship with Chris. She's started telling him
she has to work late when she is really seeing Laurie
to avoid conflict. But Xia doesn't like being dishon-
est either.*

*Chris can intuitively tell something is up when Xia
hides things from him, and it's creating insecurity and
jealousy on his end. He wonders if there's more going
on that he doesn't know about.*

WHAT'S GOING ON

Xia needs to feel safe so she can tell Chris things without fear. Chris needs to work on both his reception of this information and his willingness to sit with discomfort if he is unhappy about Laurie's presence in their lives. There needs to be room for some disappointment in a relationship and an ability to sit with that disappointment, otherwise couples may turn to deception to avoid that discomfort.

If you or your partner find yourselves being deceitful in your relationship, consider it a sign that your boundaries need reworking. Think about what you need from each other to feel safe being honest moving forward. The dynamics in couples that have ongoing deceit may be really difficult to reverse without professional help.

ADDRESS THE ISSUE

1. Before starting, do a quick scan of both of your physical and mental states. Does one of you feel hungry or tired/exhausted? If yes, address those basic needs first and make an appointment to regroup.

2. Find a quiet space without distractions. It might be good to get outside of your house and go to the park or even talk in the car.

3. Use Skill #1: Building Awareness of Your Defaults (page 13), Skill #2: Identifying Reactivity (page 20), and Skill #3: Learning to Interrupt Reactivity (page 24) to better understand both partners' default settings about difficult conversations.

continued →

4. The person in Chris's shoes can use Skill #14: Separating Thoughts from Feelings (page 77) to separate their thoughts or judgments about the person who is in Laurie's shoes.

5. The person who identifies with Xia can focus on Skill #18: Circling Back to Repair Misunderstanding (page 92) and Skill #19: Making an Apology That Counts (page 94) to help take responsibility for any deceitful behavior and reassure both friend and partner that they'll practice honesty moving forward.

TIP Every couple has different working understandings of transparency, secrecy, and privacy. There's no one right way to handle deceit for all relationships, but it is important you and your partner are on the same page about where your boundaries are drawn.

DISCUSSION NOTES

Ask your partner:

→ What information might be okay to keep private from each other?

→ Is there anything I can do to make you feel more comfortable sharing with me?

changing plans

Alena wants to change careers and is nervous to tell her partner, Jeff. She's been supporting their household financially with her two-location hair salon business, but she's ready to do something else. Lately, she's been having a lot of anxiety about work and dreads going in.

Jeff has always been proud of Alena for her work. It's not common for someone her age to already have a salon in her name, let alone two. He feels indifferent about his own work but is grateful for a steady paycheck and benefits. He's recently started thinking about going back to school, but worries he'll let Alena down if he's not covering their health care benefits.

WHAT'S GOING ON

I see too many couples get mixed up when making decisions because they begin conversations without clear goals. This is what often transpires: we bring up a topic for discussion with our partner, it triggers their anxiety, and they begin to respond with anxiety instead of the support we were looking for. If we want to avoid conflicts like these, we have to set up a more intentional dialogue from the beginning.

In Alena and Jeff's case, neither has much experience making intentional decisions as partners. They both tend toward conflict avoidance, which means they have long spells without conflict and then occasional explosive fighting, with a laundry list of complaints surfacing.

When you talk with your partner, it helps to be clear if you are looking for input versus looking to share authority in decision-making. Let them know when you just want support and when you are looking for co-sponsorship for your solution.

ADDRESS THE ISSUE

1. Before starting, do a quick scan of both of your physical and mental states. Does one of you feel hungry or tired/exhausted? If yes, address those basic needs first and make an appointment to regroup.

2. Find a quiet space without distractions. It might be good to get outside of your house and go to the park or even talk in the car.

3. Review Skill #12: Building Emotional Literacy (page 71) and Skill #13: Developing Empathetic Communication Skills (page 73) to set the stage for a potentially difficult conversation.

4. Consider implementing Skill #9: Recognizing Unresolvable Conflicts (page 58) to clarify your intention in starting the conversation.

5. Use Skill #11: Establishing Emotional Consent (page 66) to identify the goal for your conversation. Are you asking permission, do you want input, or is there another way your partner can show they support you? Having a clear goal will help you work toward it in partnership.

TIP Keep in mind that it's okay to have differences in the ways you approach big and small decisions, but you want to have ways to talk about them that feel intentional and effective.

DISCUSSION NOTES

Sit down with your partner to talk through the following reflections:

→ Tell me about a time you navigated change really well. What made it work for you?

→ How do you handle changing plans?

→ What can I do to support you through times of uncertainty if they ever come up?

→ What is your personal passion? What legacy do you hope to leave with your work?

→ How can I support your career dreams and professional passions? How can I support your creativity?

9

· · · · ·

FINANCES

FINANCIAL PROBLEMS in relationships can be especially difficult to address because so much of our self-worth is tied to our professional life and our income. In this chapter, we'll discuss some of the most common financial obstacles and tensions couples face, and use the skills we've covered to help resolve them.

financial upbringing

Alex was brought up in an upper-middle-class setting. She never thought she was well-off, but when she and Darla got serious, it started to become clear their upbringings were very different, and it was impacting the way they each expected to share financial information in the relationship.

Alex's family never talked about money growing up. They had very little financial stress, and her parents seemed to take care of financial worries without the children's knowledge. Darla knew when her family was doing okay and when things were tight in graphic detail. Her parents shared very openly whenever they were stressed about money.

They came to my office because even though they felt strong in all other areas of the relationship, they simply couldn't talk about money without an emotional explosion.

WHAT'S GOING ON

There are three key differences impacting this couple's ability to communicate about money, namely: exposure to financial information, role modeling, and experience talking about money. Alex had little exposure to any of this while Darla learned at a young age just how difficult financial struggles could be for a family.

Most couples have very different default settings related to money, information sharing, and financial decision-making. By learning to understand these default settings, couples can close communication gaps and function much more effectively as a financial team.

There's nothing inherently wrong with your relationship if you handle money differently. But you want to be sure you can talk about your preferences and insecurities in ways that bring stronger understandings instead of divisions.

ADDRESS THE ISSUE

1. Before starting, do a quick scan of both of your physical and mental states. Does one of you feel hungry or tired/exhausted? If yes, address those basic needs first and make an appointment to regroup.

2. Find a quiet space without distractions. It might be good to get outside of your house and go to the park or even talk in the car.

3. Revisit Skill #6: Creating a Secure Space for Vulnerability (page 44) and talk about how to create safety for each of you and your vulnerability around financial conversations.

4. Implement Skill #17: Understanding Your Conflict Dance (page 87) before further tense conversations, and grow your understanding of your conflict patterns.

5. Partners are more likely to feel heard and understood if they try Skill #12: Building Emotional Literacy (page 71) and Skill #15: Following Up (page 80) to challenge themselves to really listen with empathy as their partner shares concerns or insecurities about money.

TIP Our cultural norms tell us successful couples meld all their finances, but there's very little data showing us that this practice is any more successful than keeping some financial responsibilities separate. There is no one-size-fits-all financial plan for successful relationships; just be clear and confident in your decisions together.

DISCUSSION NOTES

Consider your own background and how it could be different than your partner's experience. Use the questions below to share some of your early life reflections:

→ What was your experience of having more than enough growing up?

→ What was your experience of having just enough?

→ What was your experience of not having enough while growing up?

decision-making & power with money

Maggie has always been careful with money. She has been saving for retirement since her first job right after college and has maintained a near-perfect credit rating. Her boyfriend, Jeremy, on the other hand, has been less careful and learned some financial lessons the hard way.

Maggie and Jeremy came to my office because discussions about combining finances, sharing a lease, and buying a car together had gotten so tense that they needed a mediator to help them through their issues.

WHAT'S GOING ON

Maggie and Jeremy have developed different tactics for dealing with scarcity in their lives. While neither of them is doing anything wrong, they need to find a way to join together instead of having this issue divide them and leave them feeling insecure or misunderstood.

It can feel extremely vulnerable for some people to combine finances. Before you decide to do that, you need to have a discussion addressing the concerns of each partner to ensure this is a comfortable decision. It's also important for you to reflect on why sharing finances is important or meaningful to you both. There's no requirement for couples to combine funds, especially if it's something that is outside your comfort zone. There are a lot of ways to formalize your relationship without joint accounts.

ADDRESS THE ISSUE

1. Before starting, do a quick scan of both of your physical and mental states. Does one of you feel hungry or tired/exhausted? If yes, address those basic needs first. Make an appointment to regroup.

2. Find a quiet space without distractions. It might be good to get outside of your house and go to the park or even talk in the car.

3. Start by utilizing Skill #10: Giving the Benefit of the Doubt (page 62) and Skill #8: Practicing Gratitude to Deepen Emotional Intimacy (page 53) to set a tone of positive connection and gratitude.

4. Work through Skill #12: Building Emotional Literacy (page 71) and Skill #15: Following Up (page 80) to help improve overall communication.

continued →

5. Circle back to Skill #7: Moving from Judgment to Curiosity (page 49) to try to see things from each other's perspective.

TIP Smart financial conversations often involve time to reflect and gather information. Make sure you and your partner build in time for the steps above so that you can make the right decision.

DISCUSSION NOTES

Ask yourselves how your hopes and concerns are related to sharing financial accounts.

→ How could sharing financial responsibilities serve or support you individually and together?

→ If you combine funds, how will you make decisions about surprise costs, profits, and spending plans?

→ If you keep funds separate, how do you plan to consult each other on surprise costs or future expenditures?

household contribution

Camden has always been an artist at heart, and Yola loves his creativity and vision for artistic activism. So, when Cam lost his day job last year, they decided it was a sign from the universe that he should focus more on his artistic passion.

At first, they were both excited about all the creative projects Cam was able to invest in. But very quickly, Yola started noticing his artwork was prioritized over the responsibilities they shared at home. She needed to find a way to support his new career path while still wanting more support from him around the house.

WHAT'S GOING ON

Most couples fail to discuss expectations around household management effectively. And when life changes happen that can shift household duties, these unclear expectations come to the fore. Without clear boundaries or expectations, resentment can set in fast.

If you don't think you're doing more than your fair share, you're probably not doing enough. The couples who find a solid balance are ones where both partners think they're contributing to more than half the workload.

Look at your household roles and responsibilities and take stock of your individual strengths, priorities, and interests when assigning tasks rather than doing things from a place of assumption or obligation.

ADDRESS THE ISSUE

1. Before starting, do a quick scan of both of your physical and mental states. Does one of you feel hungry or tired/exhausted? If yes, address those basic needs first and make an appointment to regroup.

2. Find a quiet space without distractions. It might be good to get outside of your house and go to the park or even talk in the car.

3. Revisit Skill #20: Building Trust by Following Through (page 99) to clarify your implicit versus explicit expectations and commitments to each other.

4. To reflect on the way familial and functional intimacy is built for each of you, review Skill #24: Nourishing Functional or Familial Intimacy (page 114), so you can deepen intimacy in meaningful ways.

5. Discuss Skill #16: Shifting from Blame to Personal Accountability (page 83) as it relates to each of your shared responsibilities at this point. Also, implementing Skill #19: Making an Apology That Counts (page 94) can help you create new agreements as you and your partner move forward.

TIP   As your lives change over time, so will your ability to commit time or physical energy to certain tasks. Be sure you and your partner have a reliable way to circle back and check in periodically to reassign tasks and roles as needed.

DISCUSSION NOTES

Sit with your partner to discuss the following reflection questions:

→ How did your parents model responsibility sharing?

→ What did fairness look like in your household?

→ What are your strengths in taking care of our home, cars, or other shared responsibilities?

→ What are your real areas of weakness? Which tasks and responsibilities feel beyond your skill set?

→ How will you know when you need to change up some part of your shared household responsibilities?

10

. . . .

FAMILY

IT'S WELL KNOWN in our culture that in-laws cause tension for lots of couples. In this chapter, we'll discuss the ways our families create problems in relationships and walk through several common scenarios using skills to help you resolve similar issues in your own relationship.

in-laws &
family norms

Ryan and Michelle have trouble whenever they visit Michelle's sister, Tana, for Sunday dinner. At these dinners, each family member takes a turn giving updates about their week and expressing gratitude as they go around the table. Ryan says Tana "isn't terrible, but she is weird." He never feels fully comfortable at her house and would rather spend less time there.

Michelle loves her sister and would spend more time with her if she could. She's sad the two people closest to her are not connecting. Plus, the awkwardness between Ryan and Tana makes her uncomfortable, especially at family holidays that are so meaningful to her.

WHAT'S GOING ON

There might be several reasons why Ryan is not connecting with Michelle's sister, Tana. It may be rooted in their differing family norms. Ryan grew up in a family that was expressive, loud, and full of sarcasm. In his family, conflict was handled openly, directly, and almost immediately. He doesn't see his family often, but when they do, it is a loud and affectionate celebration filled with music, drinking, and games.

Sunday dinners and holidays at Tana's are more subdued affairs compared to Ryan's family. Ryan feels uncomfortable at Tana's because he reads her household as orderly and unexpressive. And although she hasn't said it to him yet, Michelle is usually overwhelmed by all the commotion when she visits his family.

There's nothing wrong with either family. The challenge with in-laws is working to understand their family norms. Every family's norms are different, just like different nations. Sometimes these norms are weird to us simply because we're not familiar with them. Try to approach your in-laws' traditions and practices with curiosity and a sense of learning instead of judging them. The more you can be open-minded, generous, and curious in your interpretation of your partner's family, the more likely you will find some commonality or way to appreciate them. That said, you are always allowed to set boundaries in relationships that feel uncomfortable to you.

ADDRESS THE ISSUE

1. Before starting, do a quick scan of both of your physical and mental states. Does one of you feel hungry or tired/exhausted? If yes, address those basic needs first and make an appointment to regroup.

2. Find a quiet space without distractions. It might be good to get outside of your house and go to the park or even talk in the car.

3. Work on Skill #6: Creating a Secure Space for Vulnerability (page 44) and Skill #11: Establishing Emotional Consent (page 66) to create an environment of safety for talking about tender issues.

4. Each partner should practice Skill #7: Moving from Judgment to Curiosity (page 49) to check if there are judgments or misperceptions getting in the way of their connection.

TIP Remember that your in-laws are family you may not have chosen, but they are yours. Try to find ways to make your time with them as enjoyable—or at least as peaceful—as possible. It might be useful to look at Skill #3: Learning to Interrupt Reactivity (page 24) to have self-soothing practices ready for situations when you must be in contact with them and Skill #26: Recognizing When Boundaries Need Work (page 121) to clarify your boundaries with your in-laws.

DISCUSSION NOTES

Remember that boundaries can change over time. Think about relationships in your life where boundaries have changed as you needed them to; then ask yourself the following questions and share your responses with your partner:

→ How did you know when it was time to change boundaries in these relationships?

→ How can you use those same senses to inform your boundaries now?

boundaries with family

Beth has always been close to her sisters, and they have a habit of sharing everything with each other. But when she and Jason started having some sexual troubles, he made her promise not to tell anyone. Over a bachelorette weekend, Beth was cornered by her sisters and grilled for details about married life. After a few glasses of wine, she let on vaguely that things hadn't been easy in the bedroom.

When she came home and told Jason what had happened, he flipped out. He felt embarrassed and expressed that he didn't want to see her sisters at Christmas.

WHAT'S GOING ON

In my office, I see very few couples who have clear boundaries about secrecy and privacy. While this is a really common oversight, I recommend talking about these topics before you reach a misunderstanding instead of operating on assumption alone. In particular, partners can often have a different understanding of privacy boundaries when it comes to their families.

ADDRESS THE ISSUE

1. Before starting, do a quick scan of both of your physical and mental states. Does one of you feel hungry or tired/exhausted? If yes, address those basic needs first and make an appointment to regroup.

2. Find a quiet space without distractions. It might be good to get outside of your house and go to the park or even talk in the car.

3. If you are in a similar situation, before you can begin any work setting up boundaries with your partner's family, you need to repair the trust betrayal with your partner. Start with Skill #18: Circling Back to Repair Misunderstanding (page 92) and Skill #19: Making an Apology That Counts (page 94) to apologize and repair trust.

4. Once trust has been reestablished (which may take some time), work through Skill #26: Recognizing When Boundaries Need Work (page 121).

5. Review Skill #27: Differentiating among Wants, Needs, & Requirements (page 123) and Skill #28: Asking for What You Need (page 126) to help you create healthy and clear boundaries moving forward and to avoid the same problems in the future.

continued →

TIP   If this particular family issue is a tricky one for you, it's okay
      to start by resolving other wounds if needed.

DISCUSSION NOTES

When you move through something difficult as a couple, it's
always important to reflect on your learning. After you've resolved
a relationship issue, challenge yourself to contemplate what you
learned from the experience.

→   What did you learn about yourself?

→   What did you learn about your partner?

→   Knowing what you do now, what would you do differently in
    the future?

information sharing & privacy

Jose's "work wife" relationship with his colleague Allyson never bothered his wife, Quiana, until last summer. What started as a group after-work drinks outing turned into just Jose and Allyson. Allyson is having problems in her marriage and is relying heavily on Jose for support.

Quiana knows nothing is happening between them and trusts Jose completely. But she doesn't think it's okay for either of them to talk about their marital issues with other friends, and she thinks Jose has shared too much about their marriage with Allyson.

WHAT'S GOING ON

It's not uncommon for partners to have different needs for privacy. In fact, differing privacy boundaries are one of the most common areas of disagreement for couples. Typically, one partner is accused of oversharing and the other of keeping too much in. I recommend every couple work together to create a "vault" with a specific list of things they agree not to share with anyone other than their therapists. These might be about their health history, sexual vulnerabilities, or insecurities. I recommend that couples create a list of what belongs in the vault, including any items that seem obvious ("I will never share your trauma history without your permission.").

In addition, it's okay to ask about your partner's friendships; it's one more way to get to know your partner. Try to focus your interest on your partner rather than learning about the other person. Instead of asking "What's she like?" ask questions like, "What kinds of things do you two have in common?" Focusing too hard on the other person misses the opportunity to connect with your partner.

ADDRESS THE ISSUE

1. Before starting, do a quick scan of both of your physical and mental states. Does one of you feel hungry or tired/exhausted? If yes, address those basic needs first and make an appointment to regroup.

2. Find a quiet space without distractions. It might be good to get outside of your house and go to the park or even talk in the car.

3. To ground yourselves before working on a tender topic like this one, apply Skill #30: Using a Mindful Approach to Conflict (page 131).

4. Revisit Skill #26: Recognizing When Boundaries Need Work (page 121) to have a meaningful conversation about the boundaries you need to adopt or clarify in relation to information you want to share with others.

5. Skill #15: Following Up (page 80) can help both partners clarify boundaries so they can move forward confidently on the same page.

TIPS   We often think of boundaries as fixed, but our boundaries have to grow and evolve with us over time. Couples who last are those who can successfully address their changing boundaries over time.

I see lots of couples who (sometimes mistakenly) assume they share definitions of monogamy, infidelity, and the fine line between friendship and relationship. I recommend talking about these definitions to ensure you're on the same page with your partner.

DISCUSSION NOTES

Together with your partner, create a "vault" of topics, stories, or terms you want to keep private. Get specific and list everything you'd rather never share without each other's permission.

In addition, you both can identify one safe outlet to get support if needed. Typically, that can be a therapist or coach who would honor confidentiality.

differing social needs

Karli has always been outgoing. She was the team captain of many sports in high school and to this day leads tons of volunteer projects outside work. She takes pride in creating groups of cohesive friends who enjoy balancing work and play. As a result, she's out often, attending events and spending time with friends.

Neil, on the other hand, has always been more of an introvert. He respects Karli's need for social time but would rather be home with the dog and one of his favorite books. In his words, "I'm just a quiet guy."

While they respect their different needs, how they like to spend time differs immensely. These differences are starting to drive a wedge between them. Neil can't understand why Karli needs so much time out, and Karli wishes he shared more of her social interests.

WHAT'S GOING ON

This is a great example of a couple's default settings being different. Their baseline needs for social interaction are dissimilar. There's no right or wrong way to be (introverted or extroverted); they're just different preferences.

Often, when our defaults are very different, we can sink into a judgmental mindset. Our judgments can harden into resentments if we don't employ skills to soften them.

It's not at all unusual for couples to have different needs for social connection. You can address this by checking in regularly with your schedules and discussing the kinds of social energy output anticipated over the course of the coming week. This way, you can plan for quiet time together before or after overstimulating gatherings. It can also give you time to find a friend to go with you if your partner needs to opt out for an event.

Remember, the health of your relationship is not defined by whether you share similar personality traits (extroversion or introversion), but from the way you support each other in meeting social needs.

ADDRESS THE ISSUE

1. Before starting, do a quick scan of both of your physical and mental states. Does one of you feel hungry or tired/exhausted? If yes, address those basic needs first and make an appointment to regroup.

2. Find a quiet space without distractions. It might be good to get outside of your house and go to the park or even talk in the car.

continued →

3. Practice perspective-taking by using Skill #13: Developing Empathetic Communication Skills (page 73), Skill #14: Separating Thoughts from Feelings (page 77), and Skill #15: Following Up (page 80).

4. Also practice Skill #9: Recognizing Unresolvable Conflicts (page 58) to determine if this is a resolvable conflict for you.

5. Revisit Skill #7: Moving from Judgment to Curiosity (page 49) to set aside judgments if they're creating distance between you.

TIP Challenge yourself to stay open and present with your partner's responses to these skill practices. Learning any new skill is going to take practice, but the more you two try to learn from mistakes along the way, the better integrated the skill becomes.

DISCUSSION NOTES

Sometimes when we have trouble understanding our partner, our perceptions and stories are less about them than they are about us. Next time you notice yourself interpreting your partner negatively, ask yourself if there's any part of your criticism that is actually more about you.

reaffirming the couple bubble

Nels and Annika always end up fighting the whole way home after they visit her folks. Annika's mom often picks passive-aggressive fights with Nels. As a result, the couple feels like they're pitted against each other when it comes to Annika's mom. It has become a real issue since they moved closer to home and Annika's parents invite them for dinner every Sunday night.

They feel obligated to attend but hate the way they feel, leaving tense and disconnected.

WHAT'S GOING ON

Stan Tatkin, a highly respected couples therapist and founder of the psychobiological approach to couples therapy (PACT), discusses "the couple bubble" as a felt sense that you're on a solid team with your partner. It gets tested when couples are around other people, and we reinforce it with small acts that reassure our sweetheart "we're in this together." Reminding yourselves just how important this sense of teamwork is for a partnership can help you start reinforcing it proactively.

If there are certain spaces or people who often test your sense of teamwork, do your best to anticipate them together with your partner so you can talk through ways to have each other's backs when you face those situations. In Nels and Annika's case, they need to identify ways they can reaffirm their bubble at these family dinners.

ADDRESS THE ISSUE

1. Before starting, do a quick scan of both of your physical and mental states. Does one of you feel hungry or tired/exhausted? If yes, address those basic needs first and make an appointment to regroup.

2. Find a quiet space without distractions. It might be good to get outside of your house and go to the park or even talk in the car.

3. To clarify what meaningful support could look like for you outside your couple bubble, revisit Skill #6: Creating a Secure Space for Vulnerability (page 44).

4. Work on Skill #8: Practicing Gratitude to Deepen Emotional Intimacy (page 53) to gracefully reconnect and affirm your couple bubble.

TIP   Your relationship's wellness is not defined by the frequency of your conflicts but by the severity of their impact. Research shows us that plenty of high-conflict couples are deeply connected, committed, and in love. The difference between them and unsuccessful couples is their ability to resolve conflicts without harming the relationship.

DISCUSSION NOTES

There are lots of ways to reinforce your bubble as a couple. Begin a conversation with your sweetheart about the times in your partnership when you felt they really had your back. What happened? What did they do or say? How did it feel in your body when that happened? What did it mean to you?

11

· · · · · · · · ·

HOME

THERE ARE SEVERAL common struggles couples face when sharing a home and building a household together. In this chapter, we'll walk through five of the most common challenges we face in live-in relationships and how you can work through them in your own partnership.

default responsibilities

Lance is starting to regret moving in with Brittany. He envisioned them having an enjoyable, relaxed atmosphere in their new place and equitably sharing the not-so-fun parts of keeping a home running. Somehow, though, he's ended up being the only one who ever cleans the apartment. It's as though Brittany doesn't see how messy the place has gotten. Lance wonders if this relationship can really last if Brittany doesn't start pitching in to do her share.

Brittany, on the other hand, can't understand why Lance gets so upset about so many little things around their apartment. To her, the apartment looks clean enough, and she thinks she's doing an okay job. She wishes Lance would lighten up. She'd rather be doing things on the weekend than spending it cleaning (as he recently suggested).

WHAT'S GOING ON

Most couples move in together without ever discussing their expectations or strengths in managing a household. Once they are settled into their new place, there's often some surprising discovery about each partner's expectations for cleanliness, quietness, and other personal preferences.

To remedy this, I ask couples to investigate their default settings as they relate to cleanliness and shared space. There's usually a lot to learn there.

For Lance and Brittany, it became clear their vastly different upbringings created very different practices in maintaining a home. Lance had been raised by parents who hired a cleaner on a weekly schedule while Brittany grew up often homeless or living with friends of her mother. She had few responsibilities related to cleaning and had little input about caring for the households they lived in.

ADDRESS THE ISSUE

1. Before starting, do a quick scan of both of your physical and mental states. Does one of you feel hungry or tired/exhausted? If yes, address those basic needs first and make an appointment to regroup.

2. Find a quiet space without distractions. It might be good to get outside of your house and go to the park or even talk in the car.

3. Begin with Skill #10: Giving the Benefit of the Doubt (page 62). Starting a conversation from a generous place often shifts the entire tenor of the talk.

4. Work through Skill #26: Recognizing When Boundaries Need Work (page 121) so you can start a practice of identifying when boundaries need work.

Remember that each of these skills takes practice. Even some of the simplest-seeming tools need practice in a variety of neutral situations before we'll fully integrate them in our more tender or tense moments.

It's okay to have a different perspective than your partner about what's important around the house, but you want to have a compassionate way to see through the differences to understand each other.

DISCUSSION NOTES

When you discuss household responsibilities with your partner, first create a list of them. Then each of you can rate the responsibility, on a scale of 1 to 10, by how important it feels to you. If it's something that must be addressed immediately, it could be a 10, and if it feels nonurgent, it might be a 1.

Notice which tasks are more important to one person versus the other. Get curious about why a task is more meaningful or important to them. Understanding this could unlock greater appreciation, understanding, and togetherness.

never checking in or updating processes

When they first got together, Latasha was finishing her master's degree and Trey was working 60-hour weeks with a long commute. It made more sense for Latasha to take on extra housework with the flexibility her thesis-writing schedule gave her.

But 10 years, two kids, and a career shift later, she's now the one traveling for work four days a week while Trey works from home as a consultant. Latasha is up late cleaning, prep cooking, tucking kids in, and planning for her next workday. She needs more from Trey but isn't sure what's fair to ask. And when she asks him for help, he either seems resistant or needs her support to get things done because she's been running everything on her own for so long.

WHAT'S GOING ON

There are lots of partnerships where we replicate the roles our parents modeled for us. Latasha's mom had always over-functioned even for her extended family, and Latasha had unknowingly picked up the same role.

She also has famously high standards of perfection, which is where she and Trey differ. While he has always been an involved father and doting husband, their household runs completely as Latasha likes it. Most of the time when Trey steps in, Latasha chastises him or takes over when he's halfway through his task. He feels minimized and has stopped trying to offer support.

Latasha is trapped between her need for partnership and her unwillingness to give up control over the household.

Most couples fall into default patterns like Latasha and Trey without ever considering them or realizing it until they've outgrown the systems that once worked well. Finding a way to regularly reflect on your needs and check in about your partner's needs can help you stay ahead of bitterness and tailor household processes to your strengths as they change with time.

ADDRESS THE ISSUE

1. Before starting, do a quick scan of both of your physical and mental states. Does one of you feel hungry or tired/exhausted? If yes, address those basic needs first and make an appointment to regroup.

2. Find a quiet space without distractions. It might be good to get outside of your house and go to the park or even talk in the car.

3. Since this can be a hot-button issue, start with Skill #3: Learning to Interrupt Reactivity (page 24) to separate thoughts from feelings. All too often household

continued →

responsibilities can be attached to misperceptions for long-term couples. Clearing those up will help you get started.

4. Review Skill #26: Recognizing When Boundaries Need Work (page 121) so you can more quickly identify when your boundaries need attention.

5. Begin making clearer requests of your partner, by applying Skill #28: Asking for What You Need (page 126).

TIP   It is really challenging to maintain a healthy romantic partnership and a functioning household at the same time. Managing household responsibility is one of the greatest sources of strife in adult relationships. If you're struggling to talk about these issues, you're not alone. But letting them go unaddressed too long will lead to resentment and contempt. Don't let that happen to you.

DISCUSSION NOTES

One of the most important practices I share with couples is a regular check-in meeting to manage responsibilities and tasks. Couples meet once a week to discuss schedules, finances, and shared resources as well as responsibilities and tasks.

Having regular check-ins helps keep any logistical conversations out of your date night. It also carves out time so you can both be fully present and removes any feeling that one person is nagging the other one. Check-ins also allow you to revisit whether specific roles or responsibilities still work for you.

Discuss with your partner what would make it possible for you to schedule a regular meeting like this. In my work, the couples who commit to these meetings have a nearly 50 percent decrease in smaller conflicts throughout the week.

no accountability or follow-through

Dawn hates it when Lea leaves her used tea bag on the counter or when she leaves trash in their shared car. And sometimes, it seems like Lea isn't thinking about Dawn. For example, she will pick up lunch only for herself when she knows Dawn is working from home, or she will make a tuna fish sandwich and not clean the dishes right away even though she knows Dawn hates the smell of it.

Lea, meanwhile, is clueless to the laundry list of irritations and resentments Dawn is growing. She notices Dawn has been a little cold lately and doesn't know how to start a thaw.

WHAT'S GOING ON

Dawn and Lea are missing an accountability process they can both work through. Dawn has plenty to upset her but has been avoiding tender conversations with Lea for months. Her avoidance hasn't resolved the issue, and over time, these tiny annoyances have grown. Dawn needs to start identifying and addressing these issues earlier—when they're small, before they expand. Lea needs to start paying closer attention to her partner and checking in about Dawn's experience so they can be back on the same page. Even if she doesn't see things the same way, it's important she can see things through Dawn's eyes and validate her concerns to create a feeling of unity in the relationship.

ADDRESS THE ISSUE

1. Before starting, do a quick scan of both of your physical and mental states. Does one of you feel hungry or tired/exhausted? If yes, address those basic needs first and make an appointment to regroup.

2. Find a quiet space without distractions. It might be good to get outside of your house and go to the park or even talk in the car.

3. The partner who most relates to Dawn should look over Skill #10: Giving the Benefit of the Doubt (page 62) to start extending a generous interpretation to their partner. They should also revisit Skill #16: Shifting from Blame to Personal Accountability (page 83) to own their part of the conflict—withholding information from the other.

4. For the other partner (the "Lea" so to speak), I suggest reviewing Skill #13: Developing Empathetic Communication Skills (page 73) to help them be open to their partner's perspective more frequently.

5. Both partners can work on Skill #26: Recognizing When Boundaries Need Work (page 121) and Skill #28: Asking for What You Need (page 126) to create stronger boundaries and learn how to communicate them in order to avoid this pattern in the future.

TIPS Clients often ask, "Is this a reasonable concern?" when they want validation that their irritation is real. The truth is, reasonable or not, it's impacting your partnership. If it's bothering you, get your issue out in the open so you can both work to understand and resolve it.

Sometimes, I hear one of the partners tell the other their concerns are unreasonable. Invalidating your partner's experience will get you nowhere. Practice validating their experience and try to see things from their perspective, even if you don't agree or if you would handle things differently.

DISCUSSION NOTES

Ask yourself the following questions and then share with your partner when you're ready:

→ A time I received hard feedback and it went well was . . .

→ What the other person/people did in the situation that helped it go smoothly was . . .

→ What I did in the situation to help it go smoothly was . . .

→ How the environment helped it be a constructive conversation was . . .

→ What I learned or changed as a result . . .

→ What that experience taught me about receiving feedback was . . .

→ How that can apply to our conflicts is . . .

request expectation management

Nadia knows she's asked Marshall to call the plumber at least twice this week. She's sick of always being the one to keep track of the calls to be made and the tasks to be done to keep their home and family functioning. But Marshall keeps saying he wants to be a reliable partner, and Nadia knows he's sick of her nagging. The last thing she wants to be in this relationship is a nag, but she fears that's what she's becoming. Nadia and Marshall come to me when they both start noticing this nagging pattern is dragging them down.

WHAT'S GOING ON

Typically, neither partner is happy with this kind of situation. Nobody wants to be a "nag." And nobody likes feeling pressured to micromanage their adult partner. When a couple tells me there's an issue with nagging, it's a clear sign to me that accountability and reliability are issues for the couple. We need a way to address and resolve a lack of follow-through before trust is broken.

It's okay to feel frustrated when your partner drops the ball. For most of us, it can eat away slowly at the trust between us and fuels resentment. But if we want to avoid resentment (a real cancer for relationships), we have to find a way to work through it—to rebuild reliability. Practice self-empathy, knowing it's okay to feel the way you do as you work to address accountability issues with your partner. Your ability to empathize with yourself will help you soften your approach with your sweetheart.

ADDRESS THE ISSUE

1. Before starting, do a quick scan of both of your physical and mental states. Does one of you feel hungry or tired/ exhausted? If yes, address those basic needs first and make an appointment to regroup.

2. Find a quiet space without distractions. It might be good to get outside of your house and go to the park or even talk in the car.

3. In this situation, a review of Skill #20: Building Trust by Following Through (page 99) is a good place to start. Utilizing this skill helps clarify the promises and agreements each partner is making to the other.

continued →

4. Next, Skill #12, Making an Apology That Counts (page 94) is very important in dealing with this issue because it helps resolve any prior conflicts about follow-through, consistency, or reliability.

TIP   Cut yourself and your partner some slack. We're only human, and it's not possible to be in a long-term relationship without dropping the ball once in a while. It's when we don't address the issue and work to change future behaviors that this becomes a problem for couples.

DISCUSSION NOTES

Reflect on the following questions. Share your thoughts with your partner when you're ready.

→ **What tools help you improve your follow-through and reliability in partnership?**

→ **What would help you avoid overpromising or overcommitting in this relationship?**

→ **When do you feel safe to make mistakes? What could your partner do to help you feel supported when you screw up?**

building resentments

*"Every time we get into a fight, he walks away,"
Kristin says about her boyfriend, Nick. "I don't know
what happens, but he just shuts down and withdraws
himself. Then I never know how to bring it up, and
nothing ever gets resolved. There's a mountain of
issues we've never tackled."*

*I see couples like Kristin and Nick every week in the
office. Every couple has a handful of hot-button
issues, but in their case, Nick shuts down conversations so quickly that it's hard for them to even tell me
which topics need the most attention. Kristin says
every time she starts a conversation about something
she wants to fix, improve, or even just explore, Nick
gets quiet and withdraws until ultimately he says,
"Let's talk about this later." He then retreats to work
or their bedroom.*

WHAT'S GOING ON

In every relationship, there's one partner who withdraws, shuts down, or stonewalls in an argument more quickly than the other. In this pair, it's Nick. It's common for one partner to feel overwhelmed really quickly when things get heated. Nick feels responsible when Kristin is unhappy, so any complaint from her feels like a direct attack.

Typically, "retreaters" wall themselves off in order to avoid feeling ashamed and guilty. But often, the more that this person backs away, the stronger their partner's approach becomes. For Kristin, this can mean she ends up yelling or crying (or both). This intensity only makes things worse and causes the other person to withdraw further as the volume rises. Many couples know this cycle all too well.

This dynamic is present at some level in nearly every relationship. Knowing which roles you tend to fall into can help you and your partner identify when you need to make a change or take a break from the conversation.

ADDRESS THE ISSUE

1. Before starting, do a quick scan of both of your physical and mental states. Does one of you feel hungry or tired/ exhausted? If yes, address those basic needs first and make an appointment to regroup.

2. Find a quiet space without distractions. It might be good to get outside of your house and go to the park or even talk in the car.

3. Use Skill #17: Understanding Your Conflict Dance (page 87) to map out your conflict pattern. What can you learn from drawing it out as a flow chart?

4. Partners who tend to retreat from tension can practice Skill #18: Circling Back to Repair Misunderstanding (page 92) to learn to return to tough issues after stepping away to decompress.

5. The other partner can work on Skill #12: Building Emotional Literacy (page 71) and Skill #14: Separating Thoughts from Feelings (page 77) to help interrupt and slow their own reactivity before their partner feels the need to withdraw.

TIP   There is nothing wrong with pausing a difficult conversation to self-soothe and manage reactivity. Just remember to circle back (Skill #18, page 92) to ensure you're reaching resolution instead of growing resentments.

DISCUSSION NOTES

Use the following questions for reflection and then share with your partner:

→ What lessons about resentment were you taught overtly or covertly by observing your parents' relationship(s)?

→ How and when were you aware of their resentments? How do you think they dealt with them?

→ In what ways are your behaviors similar to theirs?

12

· · · · · · · · · · ·

FRIENDSHIPS & OTHER PEOPLE

HEALTHY RELATIONSHIPS REQUIRE a supportive community of family and friends to help them grow. But navigating relationships with friends, colleagues, and exes can get tricky for many couples. This chapter will focus on how to talk about managing friendships with other people in ways that bring you together instead of dividing you.

no autonomy

Every time I meet a new couple, I ask about their independent social life. For Dan and Andy, they respond like many couples I work with: "We never go out on our own. All our friends are shared friends."

While Dan and Andy have a huge social network through their volunteer activities and their small business, they are in each other's presence nearly 24/7. Since their wedding two years ago, their lives have overlapped at work, at home, and socially.

They've come to see me because, in spite of all their time together, they've grown a little distant and they want to bring the spark back. They're proud to say they are best friends who do everything together. But until this moment, they've never considered that all that time together could be part of the problem.

WHAT'S GOING ON

It's obviously great for couples to like to spend time together. However, in order to maintain a truly healthy relationship, it's important you each have a little space for independence and autonomy as well. I ask every couple I work with to consider the balance of the time they spend together, social time they spend with others, and time they get to be alone. If those seem out of balance (and they almost always are), they need to take action to resolve it.

All too often, the couples who haven't invested time in individual adventures and friendships become bored with each other and themselves. They need a little autonomy to keep mystery and intrigue (key ingredients in desire) alive in their relationship. Nurturing independent interests will improve desire in your partnership by fueling your independence and by creating room for mystery between you. Yes, even if your activity is golf.

ADDRESS THE ISSUE

1. Before starting, do a quick scan of both of your physical and mental states. Does one of you feel hungry or tired/exhausted? If yes, address those basic needs first and make an appointment to regroup.

2. Find a quiet space without distractions. It might be good to get outside of your house and go to the park or even talk in the car.

3. Review Skill #22: Cultivating Physical Intimacy (page 107); Skill #23: Emotional, Spiritual, & Intellectual Intimacy (page 111); Skill #24: Nourishing Functional or Familial Intimacy (page 114), and Skill #25: Identifying Intimacy Needs in Relationships (page 117). Discuss how you increase learning, inspiration, or familial intimacy outside

of your relationship in order to support your individual and shared growth.

4. Work through Skill #7: Moving from Judgment to Curiosity (page 49) and Skill #8: Practicing Gratitude to Deepen Emotional Intimacy (page 53). These skills will help clarify your needs for other friendships and the sorts of independent adventures or learning you want to invest in.

TIP   Make the effort to stay connected to friends and family. Maintaining these additional relationships takes time and energy, but it is healthy for couples to have a community of friends and family that supports them. Challenge yourself to connect directly with one good friend every week.

DISCUSSION NOTES

Use the following questions for reflection and then share with your partner:

→   How have you compromised your individuality in this relationship?

→   How could you safely reclaim some of your autonomy in the coming month?

→   Where could you invest time or energy in your personal identity in the coming weeks?

isolation

Jill decided to stop working shortly after she and her partner, Leo, had their second child. Jill had always thought of herself as a career woman and was surprised when the idea of being a stay-at-home mom was so appealing. Fortunately, Leo's work-from-home career afforded them lots of flexibility and meant they could spend more time as a family.

Over the years, though, their home-centered family life has left them feeling a bit isolated. Neither Jill nor Leo has colleagues they connect with regularly, and there are full weeks in the winter where neither of them leaves the house.

Their isolation has left them feeling highly connected to each other but lacking in independence and outside support for their own and their family's well-being.

WHAT'S GOING ON

It's always great to hear that a couple likes each other and has a strong friendship. However, far too many couples fall into the trap of letting other relationships lapse that can come from liking each other too much. Over time, this causes isolation and eventually creates a pressure cooker for the relationship's tension—with nowhere to release.

A couple who relies too heavily only on each other can often find themselves isolated and without support when they face challenges.

It can be particularly easy for couples to become isolated when they have young children. Challenging yourself to get out and meet other families through daycare co-ops, parenting groups, play dates, and local family events helps to break out of isolation.

ADDRESS THE ISSUE

1. Before starting, do a quick scan of both of your physical and mental states. Does one of you feel hungry or tired/exhausted? If yes, address those basic needs first and make an appointment to regroup.

2. Find a quiet space without distractions. It might be good to get outside of your house and go to the park or even talk in the car.

3. Review Skill #22: Cultivating Physical Intimacy (page 107) and Skill #23: Emotional, Spiritual, & Intellectual Intimacy (page 111) to help both of you get clear about your current experience of intimacy and your desire to increase specific kinds of intimacy between you.

continued →

4. Also, work through Skill #24: Nourishing Functional or Familial Intimacy (page 114) and Skill #25: Identifying Intimacy Needs in Relationships (page 117) to discuss the intimacy needs you could each explore outside your relationship. How could you increase learning, inspiration, or familial intimacy in order to support your individual and shared growth?

TIP   Make it a priority to nurture relationships with family and friends. Maintaining those additional friendships takes time and energy, but it is healthy and beneficial for couples to have a community who supports them. Continue to challenge yourself to connect directly with one good friend every week.

DISCUSSION NOTES

Can't think of a friend to connect with? Then it's time to meet some new ones. Go to a meetup event, join a club or team, volunteer, or take up a hobby to find folks with shared interests. Make your search for new friends part of your daily life, and put effort into connecting and making new contacts wherever you go.

Ask your partner to support you. This might mean encouraging you to go out, taking on household responsibilities to give you more free time, or helping you find and choose events to attend.

jealousy

Juneau saw a message from Keith's ex pop up on his phone the other night. They've talked about his relationship with his ex before, and while Juneau does trust Keith when he says there's nothing going on, something about seeing that name on his phone has left Juneau riding waves of insecurity and jealousy. She knows they're committed and monogamous, but still she's lost sleep and been irritable ever since.

Juneau tells me she feels crazy because logically she knows nothing is going on, but part of her is still highly agitated and jealous. They've come into my office together to see how they can reassure Juneau without infringing on Keith's privacy and friendships.

WHAT'S GOING ON

Lots of couples struggle to talk about their past relationships. For many people, it's a tender topic because jealousy can be an issue and miscommunication can easily trip us up when we try to discuss the situation.

We might still be carrying feelings from past relationships, or we might be wary about making the same mistakes that we've seen in our parents' or friends' relationships, but feelings of jealousy and insecurity are easy hot-button issues for most couples.

Most of us never talk about our past relationships because, frankly, they can be so hard to discuss. We may seem like open books to our partners in so many ways, but then when it comes to our ex, we clam up. This incongruence in behavior is often more triggering to our current partner than anything we could share about our past.

Couples facing this difficulty need to find a way to talk about past partners in a manner that supports the connection and security of the current partnership.

ADDRESS THE ISSUE

1. Before starting, do a quick scan of both of your physical and mental states. Does one of you feel hungry or tired/exhausted? If yes, address those basic needs first and make an appointment to regroup.

2. Find a quiet space without distractions. It might be good to get outside of your house and go to the park or even talk in the car.

3. Begin to manage the reactive emotions this situation brings up by working on Skill #2: Identifying Reactivity (page 20) and Skill #3: Learning to Interrupt Reactivity (page 24).

4. Most of us experience some sort of distorted thinking when we feel jealous or insecure in relationships. Before addressing these thoughts with your partner, refer to Skill #4: Stopping Distorted Thinking (page 30) and Skill #5: Managing Tough Emotions with Discernment (page 37) to identify which thoughts you truly want to work on with your partner's help.

5. Focus on Skill #28: Asking for What You Need (page 126) to identify any boundaries you want or need to clarify.

6. When you are ready to have a productive, intentional conversation about your partner's history, refer to Skill #9: Recognizing Unresolvable Conflicts (page 58).

TIP It's okay to feel intense emotions, but be careful how you decide to act on them. Just because you feel something intensely does not mean you get to treat your partner poorly. If you're facing strong feelings that are hard to manage in healthy ways, it's okay to hire a therapist to help you get a handle on your emotional reactivity.

DISCUSSION NOTES

Jealousy is a normal emotional experience. The key is not to ignore it, otherwise it can grow into resentment or distance in your partnership. Instead, take time to get to know your jealousy and what it needs. For example, in a jealous moment, you might think, "I bet he likes spending time with her more than me." This might mean you need reassurance that he likes the time he's sharing with you.

Practice Skill #13: Developing Empathetic Communication Skills (page 73) to help you identify the stories and perceptions most common in your experience of jealousy.

insecurity

Brad and Lauren decided nine years ago that marriage was just not an institution they supported. They've been monogamous and living together for nearly a decade. While highly committed, they continue to feel confident that legal marriage isn't the route for them.

Although Brad is sure about the decision not to legally marry and knows Lauren is completely into him and only him, he can't help but feel insecure every once in a while. This sometimes happens when Lauren is traveling for work. Brad feels lonely at home, and while he misses her, he starts worrying she'll find someone else. He sometimes wonders if Lauren will change her mind about him someday.

When he brings this up, Lauren gets defensive: "How could you possibly think I'd leave you?" she asks. Her defensiveness leaves Brad feeling dismissed. The more they talk about it, the more Lauren feels frustrated. She's not doing anything wrong, and she's tired of feeling like she has to reassure him so much whenever she leaves town.

WHAT'S GOING ON

It's not at all uncommon for one partner in a relationship to experience more frequent and/or intense insecurity. I often see couples where there's not necessarily a reason for insecurity, but the insecurity is alive and well.

There are many reasons some partners just have a lower tolerance for insecurity in relationships. Some professionals point to an anxious attachment style that could have formed when someone (in this case, Brad) was very young. Your attachment style is developed in relationships with your parents (or caregivers) during your childhood and informs the ways you make committed bonds through the rest of your life.

It's possible Brad might have had a highly anxious attachment with his parents that still carries over into intimate relationships today, and Lauren could have had a more avoidant or detached family experience.

Either way, it's clear that someone feeling the way Brad does needs something to clarify or affirm their partnership. Marriage isn't the only way to formalize a commitment, but without it, many couples struggle to make meaning of their commitment to each other. Finding ways to concretize your partnership that are meaningful to both of you can help resolve insecurity. It could be something formal like a written contract or symbolic like a commitment ceremony or rings. There are lots of ways unmarried couples can express deep commitment. To help this couple move forward, we need to identify what is meaningful to them.

continued →

ADDRESS THE ISSUE

1. Before starting, do a quick scan of both of your physical and mental states. Does one of you feel hungry or tired/exhausted? If yes, address those basic needs first and make an appointment to regroup.

2. Find a quiet space without distractions. It might be good to get outside of your house and go to the park or even talk in the car.

3. Work through Skill #8: Practicing Gratitude to Deepen Emotional Intimacy (page 53). Couples with a solid and specific gratitude practice often resolve insecurity issues with that practice alone.

4. Revisit Skill #14: Separating Thoughts from Feelings (page 77) to encourage you to discuss the meaning you each make of insecurity and what might help either or both of you experience a stronger sense of commitment.

TIP Lots of us can feel a little silly naming the specific actions and behaviors we perceive as committed. Try not to downplay the responses you share. If they are meaningful to you, allow yourself to communicate about them with sincerity.

DISCUSSION NOTES

Revisit Skill #2: Identifying Reactivity (page 20) and focus on your experience of insecurity in this relationship or other areas of your life. What cues does your body give you when insecurity pays you a visit? Share your reflections with your partner.

infidelity

Rashad and Ali have been together for 17 years and in a recent intimate conversation revealed they'd both had short-term affairs during their time together. Ali confessed to having had a one-night stand at a conference three years ago, and Rashad admitted sharing an online flirtation that crossed several of their monogamous boundaries about a year ago.

They asked me if the fact that they had both cheated meant they should break up. They couldn't understand how they'd both cheated when they loved each other and their life together. They wanted to find a path forward—without cheating.

WHAT'S GOING ON

When most of us discover an affair, we think it's a clear sign the relationship must end. But in truth, many couples can and do stay together after infidelity. If their vulnerability and repair of trust is handled carefully, they can come through even closer than they were before the affair happened.

In my experience, most partners pursue an affair because of a conflicting sense of self. They are often using the affair as a way to explore their desire to live a different life, and to show long-buried parts of themselves. Affairs are usually more about the individual than either of the relationships.

This was the case with Rashad and Ali. Rashad felt like he was able to relive some long-lost younger parts of himself that he'd never found a way to express with Ali. For her part, Ali felt like she could be completely selfish for one night rather than thinking about her family responsibilities all the time.

Together we walked through several of the steps below to help them stay together—which is what they both said they wanted. This isn't an easy process, and there were many times they needed to repeat skills more than once to help them reconnect. It can be nearly impossible to fully recover from an affair without professional help. I highly recommend hiring a therapist to support you through the process of repair.

ADDRESS THE ISSUE

1. Before starting, do a quick scan of both of your physical and mental states. Does one of you feel hungry or tired/ exhausted? If yes, address those basic needs first and make an appointment to regroup.

2. Find a quiet space without distractions. It might be good to get outside of your house and go to the park or even talk in the car.

3. Use Skill #6: Creating a Secure Space for Vulnerability (page 44) to come up with basic agreements on how you want to handle your conversation about infidelity.

4. Most situations of infidelity bring up strong emotional reactions, so use Skill #3: Learning to Interrupt Reactivity (page 24) to have a plan to manage your feelings and reactions during the conversation.

5. Work through Skill #13: Developing Empathetic Communication Skills (page 73) to connect with your partner's perspective through the affair.

6. Use Skill #10: Giving the Benefit of the Doubt (page 62) to help you identify when your conversation moves from a place of generosity. When that happens, it's a perfect time to take a break and circle back later (see Skill #18: Circling Back to Repair Misunderstanding, page 92).

TIP   After using the steps above to create a safer space for conversation, focus attention on all the skills in Chapter 4: Accountability & Repair (page 82) to begin rebuilding trust and moving forward.

DISCUSSION NOTES

While there are certainly ways you and your partner contributed to a dynamic where an affair was even possible, it is essential for the person who did the betraying to carefully and clearly take responsibility for their actions to help repair the relationship. Skill #19: Making an Apology That Counts (page 94) is a good place to start.

→ Ask yourself what parts were able to come alive, get renewed, or be explored when you were with the other person?

→ How did you allow yourself to show up differently in those experiences?

→ What held you back from choosing those parts of yourself to explore within a monogamous framework?

If you were the person who was betrayed in the relationship, ask yourself the following questions:

→ What parts of myself have I lost connection with?

→ Are there parts of me I want to expand, explore, or renew?

→ How can I create more space for myself and my partner to show up authentically in this partnership?

CONCLUSION

I HOPE YOU see just how common communication issues are—even for healthy couples. My hope is the more you work on your communication issues, the better you'll understand that conflict is normal, expected, and nonthreatening.

Just because we come to a relationship with different default settings or unclear requests, it doesn't mean it has to stay that way. With practice and thoughtful action, we can all improve our healthy relationship and communication skills.

Healthy couples navigate conflict with a hopeful outlook and a willingness to improve their communication skills over time. They also commit to relationship maintenance, like working through this workbook together. They know that in order to enjoy fun and romance, they need to set aside time and energy dedicated to maintaining connection and trust.

You can return to this workbook anytime to tune your skills or find guidance for specific issues. You can also return to the activities to nourish your connection and deepen the emotional intimacy you share. Doing ongoing relationship maintenance work when you're on good terms will make it much easier to implement healthy communication strategies when there's tension in the air.

The more you invest in relationship growth and conflict resolution, the more trust and intimacy increase. When this starts to happen, miscommunication occurs less frequently. In other words, as you love more, you'll fight less.

APPENDIX

feelings

ANGRY	SAD	JOYFUL	AFRAID
impatient	depleted	glad	worry
vengeful	gloomy	appreciative	dread
resentful	hopeless	compassionate	insecure
peeved	troubled	calm	scared
outraged	lonely	loving	anxious
huffy	miserable	friendly	terrified
hostile	regretful	playful	concerned
disgusted	heartbroken	grateful	nervous
judgmental	grieving	empowered	threatened
furious	longing	contemplative	wary
repulsed	wistful	confident	cautious
appalled	disappointed	proud	suspicious
rattled	heavy	confident	self-conscious
shocked	restless	energetic	apprehensive
dismayed	wistful	relaxed	guarded
exasperated	withdrawn	relieved	defensive
bitter	mournful	refreshed	tense
repulsed	downcast	peaceful	uptight
irritated	sorrowful	exhilarated	disturbed
grouchy	tearful	inspired	timid
mad	tender	powerful	shy
vengeful	melancholic	courageous	alarmed
disempowered	discouraged	excited	shocked

needs

connection

acceptance

affection

appreciation

belonging

cooperation

communication

closeness

community

companionship

compassion

consideration

consistency

empathy

inclusion

to know &
be known

to see & be seen

trust

warmth

honesty

authenticity

intimacy

love

mutuality

respect

self-respect

safety

security

stability

air

food

movement

rest

shelter

water

sexual
expression

physical
wellness

play

humor

celebration

peace

quiet

ease

beauty

awe

communion

inspiration

equality

harmony

order

autonomy

choice

space

spontaneity

balance

friendship

partnership

awareness

meaning

challenge

clarity

competence

consciousness

contribution

creativity

discovery

efficacy

effectiveness

growth

hope

learning

mourning

participation

purpose

self-expression

stimulation

to matter

understanding

integrity

presence

follow-up responses

→ Can you tell me more about that?

→ What meaning do you make of that?

→ How did you feel when that happened?

→ What changed for you when that happened?

→ I imagine you're feeling _____. Is that true for you?

→ How did/does that impact you?

→ What do you mean by _____?

→ What did you learn from that experience?

→ What were/are you hoping for in that situation?

→ What advice would you give yourself about that?

→ How do you make sense of that experience?

→ What changes when you think that?

→ What stories are you creating about that?

→ How have you tried to address this before?

→ What was your intent in that situation?

→ How do you interpret that?

→ What would you do differently if you had it to do over?

→ How did you contribute to that situation?

→ How do you want this to be different in the future?

→ How can I support you with that?

REFERENCES

general

Brown, Brené. *Daring Greatly: How the Courage to Be Vulnerable Transforms the Way We Live, Love, Parent, and Lead.* New York: Avery, 2015.

———. *I Thought It Was Just Me (but it isn't): Making the Journey from "What Will People Think?" to "I Am Enough."* New York: Avery, 2007.

Duhigg, Charles. *The Power of Habit: Why We Do What We Do in Life and Business.* New York: Random House, 2014.

Gottman, John M. *The Relationship Cure: A 5 Step Guide to Strengthening Your Marriage, Family, and Friendship.* New York: Harmony, 2002.

Lyubomirsky, Sonja. *The How of Happiness: A New Approach to Getting the Life You Want.* New York: Penguin, 2008.

Fruzzetti, Alan E. *The High-Conflict Couple: A Dialectical Behavior Therapy Guide to Finding Peace, Intimacy & Validation.* Oakland, CA: New Harbinger, 2006.

Perel, Esther. *Mating in Captivity.* London: Hodder & Stoughton, 2007.

Tatkin, Stan. *Wired for Love: How Understanding Your Partner's Brain Can Help You Defuse Conflicts and Spark Intimacy.* Oakland, CA: New Harbinger, 2012.

part one

Johnson, Sue. *Hold Me Tight: Seven Conversations for a Lifetime of Love.* New York: Little, Brown and Company, 2008.

Levine, Amir, and Rachel Heller. *Attached: The New Science of Adult Attachment and How It Can Help You Find—and Keep—Love.* New York: Tarcher, 2011.

Rosenberg, Marshall B. *Nonviolent Communication: A Language of Life.* Encinitas, CA: PuddleDancer Press, 2003.

part two

O'Hanlon, Bill. *Do One Thing Different: Ten Simple Ways to Change Your Life.* New York: HarperCollins, 1999.

Prochaska, James O., John C. Norcross, and Carlo C. DiClemente. *Changing for Good: A Revolutionary Six-Stage Program for Overcoming Bad Habits and Moving Your Life Positively Forward.* New York: William Morrow, 1994.

Siegel, Daniel J. *Mindsight: The New Science of Personal Transformation.* New York: Random House, 2010.

Stone, Douglas, Bruce Patton, and Sheila Heen. *Difficult Conversations: How to Discuss What Matters Most.* New York: Viking Penguin, 1999.

INDEX

ACKNOWLEDGMENTS

MY BELOVED, RAE, I couldn't complete this or any project without your enduring enthusiastic support. Thank you for your willingness to use our marriage as a test kitchen for my zany workbooks. I am so lucky. I love you.

My sweet children, Murphy and Lulu, you fill my heart and make dreams come true. When you come of age, I will be delighted to have you read my book.

Thanks to my parents, Rudy and Shirley, for modeling healthy loving communication for me and for generations of growing families across Wisconsin. I'm proud to be your kid.

To my sweet sister Angie, thank you for your patience. You are the inspiration behind every mention of warmth and generosity here.

Thank you to my colleagues Jeff and Julie for our playful little podcast and for all your encouragement through the writing process.

I would not have been able to write this book without the teachers who supported my learning as an early professional, especially Dr. P. B. Poorman and Camille Bertagnolli, who inspired me to pursue graduate studies and build a more loving world.

Dana, Stuke, Kate, Jenny, Kel, Casey, Effie, and Sadie: thank you for teaching me the power of emotional intimacy beyond romantic partnership.

There is no way to overstate the contribution of my clients to this work. I'm honored by your trust in me. Thank you for allowing me to inspire others with your stories.

ABOUT THE AUTHOR

GINA SENARIGHI, PhD, CPC, is an author, teacher, sexuality counselor, and certified relationship coach. She's been supporting clean fights and dirty sex in happy, healthy relationships as an educator, coach, consultant, and couples therapist for over 10 years.

Gina was named Portland's Best Life Coach in 2019 and has taught psychology courses and guest lectured on passion, alternative relationships, and sex-positive therapy at universities across the United States. Students and clients love her no-nonsense yet nonjudgmental style.

Gina currently leads couples intimacy retreats and communication workshops and coaches online clients all over the world. Her podcast, *Swoon,* has received incredible praise for its warmth and practicality. She teaches communication skills online and through in-person workshops, helping participants shift long-standing patterns to form more meaningfully connected partnerships.

She recently expanded her work to support entrepreneurial couples and cofounders to build trustworthy, courageous connections within small businesses; communicate effectively; and nurture rewarding relationships in creative ventures so they don't lose their relationship as they build their dreams.

When she's not working, you can find her in her urban garden, cuddling her tiny dog, Frida, or traveling the world with her partner, Rae, and their two beautiful children, Murphy and Lulu.